Haringey Council

# A History of

# Pantomime

# A History of Pantomime

## Maureen Hughes

PEN & SWORD HISTORY

First published in Great Britain in 2013 by
Pen & Sword History
an imprint of
Pen & Sword Books Ltd
47 Church Street
Barnsley
South Yorkshire
S70 2AS

ISBN 978 1 84468 077 1

| Haringey Libraries | | |
| --- | --- | --- |
| CC | | |
| Askews & Holts | 18-Dec-2013 | |
| 792.3809 | | |
| | HAOL3/12/13 | |

Printed and bound in the UK by CPI Group (UK) Ltd, Croydon, CRO 4YY
Typeset by Mac Style, Bridlington, East Yorkshire

Pen & Sword Books Ltd incorporates the imprints of Pen & Sword Archaeology,
Atlas, Aviation, Battleground, Discovery, Family History, History, Maritime, Military,
Naval, Politics, Railways, Select, Social History, Transport, True Crime, and
Claymore Press, Frontline Books, Leo Cooper, Praetorian Press, Remember When,
Seaforth Publishing and Wharncliffe

For a complete list of Pen & Sword titles please contact
PEN & SWORD BOOKS LIMITED
47 Church Street, Barnsley, South Yorkshire, S70 2AS, England
E-mail: enquiries@pen-and-sword.co.uk
Website: www.pen-and-sword.co.uk

# CONTENTS

For
TOM AND MARIAN HUGHES
My Wonderful Father-in-Law and Mother-in-Law

# ACKNOWLEDGEMENTS

A book doesn't write itself, it requires an author and that author in turn requires help. It might be to proofread the final manuscript; it might be to fill in some chasms of knowledge in areas generally alien to the writer in his/her everyday life. In my case it was then that I turned to my family and friends, and on some occasions complete strangers for help and it is to them that I would like to express my gratitude for their assistance in getting this book to print. And just as important, I would also like to thank my family and friends not just for their help but for always being there for me.

I'll start with my beloved family, and why not because like all families they walk beside me through thick and thin and without them being there with me then, quite frankly, I would have no reason to write. So to my husband of over thirty years, Gwyn, I want to say thank you for yet again being there to help me proofread my work, a mind-numbing task at which he is astonishingly good as he picks up the most miniscule of mistakes that I would have otherwise missed. And – he does all the cooking too, and what a chef I married, as my hips will testify! My children, Kieran and Vicky, always supportive when things get fraught and time short; when the chips are down and I needed help with a multitude of things I just have no time to do – then there they are! Vicky doing all the Christmas shopping and Kieran out with his camera taking photos for me. Thank you to the pair of you. Thank you too to my two 'special' girls, Paula and Aisha, who were always ready on the end of a phone, also willing to do anything they could to make life easier. Aisha baking amazing cakes – essential to my physical and mental well-being! – and at Christmas she wrapped all my presents for me when I ran out of time – I am kind of hoping that I can extend that help into paying for them too next year! No? Oh well, worth a try! She was also a tremendous help with preparing the index – another mind-numbing job in the life of a writer – and Paula?

Well, she is ever the voice of reason when all seems lost, always able to see the wood 'despite' the trees!

In 2010 disaster struck when I was diagnosed with cancer. Normal life was no longer normal and everything was put on hold, which included the completion of this book, as I underwent major surgery and then several gruelling courses of chemotherapy. They always say that in times of trouble people show their real colours and my word how true that statement has proved to be. Even my friends in Australia (Enda) and California (James) keep in close contact and check in with me regularly.

It was and is a difficult period in my life and I cannot thank my commissioning editor Lisa Hooson and her boss Charles Hewitt at my publishing House Pen and Sword enough for their kindness, patience and understanding during this trying time. They know that writing is my greatest joy and pass-time and frankly I thought that I would lose that joy when I became unable to meet deadlines. They would have had every reason and right to pull the plug on me and my books, which would actually have broken my heart, but no, they didn't do that but instead told me that they would wait until I was well enough to pick up where I left off. I am sure the knowledge that I had my writing waiting for me aided my recovery and so I will be forever grateful to the pair of them.

Of course, my family became my crutch and carried me heart and soul through the daily trauma, each one of them leading the way through the darkest days in their own special way, from my immediate family taking care of every day needs to my cousin Michael who listened to all my moaning and groaning; who checked on me every day to make sure I was okay and that generally there was some sun in my world. I have come to the conclusion that everyone needs a cousin Michael in their lives! I certainly couldn't imagine life without mine. I cannot name every single person, but I really must mention my two bosses, Louise Pieri and Rachel Crouch, Principals of Performance Preparation Academy where I am a teacher, who have proved themselves to be angelic in the extreme. Despite my on-going battle with cancer they have been there by my side with continual support and kindness, both giving me the drive and strength to carry on the fight. This intense care, the care shown to me, is at the very heart and cornerstone of the principles of the academy. Please let this be a lesson to everyone, 'kindness is of more value than any medication'. Rachel and Louise you are two very special people.

Now, I often hear writers, and performers for that matter, moan and groan about their agents; that's because they haven't met mine! Hilary, at Straight Line Management, used to be my agent but now she is, oh so much more. She is a very, very special friend who has shown to me the most stoic loyalty over the past few years, a loyalty I have no way of ever repaying. It was Hilary who drove me to and from my chemotherapy sessions too – my husband being forced to go to work and keep the bread buttered! So, Hilary, thank you, you are the perfect friend! I have the best family and the best friends for which I am so grateful, and thank you once again – all of you.

It doesn't end there either, for complete strangers have also been of invaluable help to me throughout the process of writing this book on Pantomime, people such as Mr Pantomime himself, Nigel Ellacott, and to be honest what he doesn't know about the Pantomime world really isn't worth knowing at all, as they say, so I really am indebted to him. He is a great and generous chap, and throughout the writing process nothing has been too much trouble for him, and as for photos, well most included in the book are courtesy of Nigel Ellacott. I am so grateful to him and if I had a magic wand, or lamp even, then I would grant him not the standard three wishes, but wishes untold.

Of course, my thanks would not be complete without including those wonderful medical experts at the Royal Marsden Hospital in London who saved my life and to those at the Royal Marsden Sutton who are now striving to extend it as much, and for as long, as they can. So, Mr Thomas Ind, my surgeon in London, and all of his team – THANK YOU, thank you for saving my life way back in 2010. And the same thanks go also to Professor Kaye and Susanna Banerjee, the specialist oncologists based in Sutton, who together with their team, have gone on to continue the fight against my cancer in order to give me as much time as possible – to write more books! And 'medical' thanks would not be complete without a mention for my wonderful GP, Dr Heather Carr-White, who takes such good care of me all year round. These are the experts, but supporting them is an entire army of dedicated staff who make up the wonderful Royal Marsden Hospital; there are too many to mention all of them, but I would like to thank the nurses in the Medical Day/IV Unit in Sutton who, every week, administer chemotherapy with such care and compassion to hundreds of patients, each desperate to win their own personal battle against cancer. And my final message of thanks is to Claire Burtenshawe, a fellow patient, whose courage and dignity has been an inspiration to me, as I am sure it has been to many other patients too.

# INTRODUCTION

Like many children, one of my first experiences of theatre was being taken to the Pantomime each year by my parents. To this day I truly believe this is an excellent, and of course enjoyable, way to introduce children to joys of theatre, and let's face it, at Christmas time it's not difficult to find a Pantomime somewhere in the UK. From village halls through to large and grand theatres, during the Christmas period Pantomimes are out there beckoning to one and all. There are even production companies dedicated to staging just Pantomimes, and there are like-minded theatre groups too whose sole purpose is the production of such to the exclusion of all other things theatrical.

There are lessons to be learned by going to the 'Pantomime' – for the storyline is always one of good triumphing over evil, which is an excellent example to set to our impressionable offspring. There are other lessons to be learned too, such as do not let excited children eat too much before the trip; do not take your elderly aunt who is not overly fond of children, for the theatre will be teeming with them and certainly do not take granny who likes a nice quiet time for with audience participation, which is all a part of the fun, quiet is not on the programme! And finally, be prepared for jokes brim full of innuendo which may affect those with more sensitive ears. Having said that though, in the well-written Pantomimes, these 'jokes' will be so well crafted that they will fly straight over the heads of little people and go unnoticed – or not understood more like – by those with, as they say, an innocent mind!

Pantomime is essentially a British thing and as confusing to tourists as cricket is to – well, everyone I suppose – but how wonderful to have a style of production that belongs to just the British; it's enough to bring out the patriot in just about anyone. Not only do we have a collection of Pantomimes that really only work in the UK, but as a result we also have a list of stock characters to whom we can all relate; in fact some of the characters names are now often used as adjectives too. Think about it, we all know that if we call someone a 'proper little Cinderella' that she is a downtrodden, goody two-shoes. You see Pantomime may seem flippant on the surface, but there are often hidden, unexplored depths.

*Disagree?*
*Just try it and see!*

## PANTOMIME QUOTATIONS

What others have thought or said about Pantomime over the years.

Pantomime is no longer what it used to be.

*The Times*, 1846

I am grim all day, but I make you laugh at night.

Joseph Grimaldi

It's bold; it's brash; it's Pantomime.

Anon

Everybody 'pooh-poohs' the Pantomime, but everybody goes to see it. It is voted 'sad nonsense' and played every night for two months.

*The Times*, 1823

Let us at once confess to a fondness for Pantomimes … we revel in Pantomimes.

Charles Dickens

What is Pantomime? Who knows, who cares? All we know is that a world without Pantomime would be like a face without a smile – grim and dismal.

Anon

Oh for an hour of Herod.

Anthony Hope, during the first performance of *Peter Pan*, 1904

Nothing is what it seems when the Pantomime magic dust falls upon the stage – animals appear to have four legs, but are actually two people; boys are girls, girls are boys, dresses can be made out of jewels or junk and the audience are a part of the cast.

Jeremy Burton

A child who has never seen a Pantomime, or an adult who has never seen a Pantomime, is a public danger.

George Bernard Shaw

To see a Pantomime is to see the ridiculous simplicity of the world through the eyes of a child.

Anon

*Chapter 1*

# WELCOME TO THE MAGICAL WORLD OF PANTOMIME

*The word Pantomime itself comes from the Greek, meaning 'We can act everything'.*

Well, I suppose I really should start at the beginning with the historical background to Pantomime, though why ever I would want to do something quite so conventional when writing about a subject so unconventional is a bit of a mystery, even to me!

## A BRIEF HISTORY OF PANTOMIME

Pantomime was originally a theatrical entertainment in which the meaning was conveyed entirely without the use of dialogue and using only gestures and bodily actions.

When asking the question 'Where did it come from?', and by 'it' at this point I am not only referring to Pantomime but in fact to anything at all, we must always keep in mind that the answer to many such questions must be based not just on fact, but on conjecture, assumptions, word of mouth, sketchy writings, etc. And, of course, when 'things' are passed down through the ages there is bound to be distortion of some sort. The reason being that information that has been passed down the centuries is liable to some extent, lesser or greater, to become a victim of the Chinese whispers problem. Of course, some historians will probably disagree with me – my son is a historian and so I am not completely naive in this area – but to them I would say that many historical 'facts' are actually theories. I rest my case, and hope that my son will forgive me! That out of the way then, I can now put to you what is generally considered to be the answer to the question: 'From where did Pantomime actually evolve?'

Panto isn't new; it dates back centuries.

The term 'Pantomime' was first used in reference to performers who presented popular, bawdy, solo, comic entertainments throughout the Roman Empire. Although this really had nothing at all to do with Pantomime as we know it today, we can actually perhaps attribute – or blame, whichever you prefer – the preoccupation with cross dressing that is prevalent in Pantomime to the ancient Greeks and Romans as, for them, cross dressing was a feature of the Bacchanalia of their times, with their slaves dressing in the clothes of their masters and mistresses. Was this the true birth of the Dame then?

In most other countries outside the UK the word Pantomime is associated with expert mime artists such as Marcel Marceau. In the UK, however, the word Pantomime conjures up an entirely different picture. So it is both interesting and sad to note that the birth of Pantomime was not in the UK, as we British like to believe. Even after the claims of the ancient Greeks and Romans, we British are still somewhat in the shadows as it would seem that the next major and significant stage in the evolvement of this theatrical experience came both from Italy and France. For it was John Weaver, a Drury Lane dancing master, who staged the *Tavern Bikers*, copying the Italian Night Scenes and which were performed by French troupes at Drury Lane in the early part of the eighteenth century. The Italian Night Scenes were comedies in which the plot was communicated to

16

the audience through the medium of slapstick and dance, rather than through dialogue, and portrayed a misunderstanding which in turn led to a comedy brawl. One of the characters in the Italian Night Scenes was much loved by playgoers, and that was Harlequin; Harlequin, by popular demand, therefore remained as an important ingredient in the Pantomime mix right up until the twentieth century.

It was, though, his production of *The Loves of Mars and Venus* in 1717 which was the first production to be actually billed as a Pantomime, so I suppose one could say then that this is where it all started. It was in the same year too that he joined John Rich, who was to dominate the early history of Pantomime, at Lincoln's Inn where the first of the Harlequinades were staged and whose idea it was to combine fairy tales with Harlequinades, thus establishing an entirely new form of theatre in which mime as such was virtually non-existent. And so we have the birth of Pantomime in the UK which then continued to develop throughout the remainder of the century. It was still, however, a long way from what we today regard as 'true' Pantomime – but from little acorns great oaks grow, and grow it did. In 1750 the celebrated David Garrick presented his first Pantomime production, proving to all that this was a particular type of theatre that was here to stay. Those then that are still determined to claim Pantomime as a British institution, both in origin and survival, could I suppose do so, given this!

It was in the 1800s that the great Joseph Grimaldi made his first appearance as a clown and that Pantomime itself became an established form of theatre in its own right. From this moment on things evolved, developed and changed as the art form grew to be what it is today and men played old women, young women played young men, animals spoke and everyone always lived happily ever after. The success of a Pantomime began to rely on the expected and not on the element of surprise. Take away the expected – which was in fact expected to happen year in and year out – and the Pantomime was a failure. And so the seeds of Pantomime tradition were sown and continue to flourish through to this day.

Pantomime is now well established as the traditional and annual form of Christmas entertainment, and is also customarily just for the children – or so they say – though why it takes five or six adults to take one child to the theatre is beyond me, unless of course this piece of children's entertainment is actually a smoke screen for the adults who are reluctant to admit their addiction to Pantomime! If you don't believe me then go to any Pantomime during the Christmas period and you will find one child accompanied by: Mum, Dad, Grandma, Grandpa and assortment of doting aunts and uncles – doting on the Pantomime, that is, and not on the child!

## WHAT MAKES A SUCCESSFUL PANTOMIME?

*To be successful one has to strive for greatness.*

Now you have some sort of idea about the background to this magical world let's open the door and enter. Pantomime is theatrical Marmite – you will either love it, or hate it! But whichever emotion Pantomime evokes in you it is, never-the-less, a form of theatre where most individuals cut their thespian teeth and so even for those averse to the enforced rituals of traditional Pantomime, they are still often indebted to its very existence as they move on to love all things theatrical. Essentially now a British tradition, it has over the years confused many an unsuspecting visitor to our shores during the Christmas period. Tourists who thought they were just going to have a night out at the theatre instead found themselves in some sort of make–believe land where everyone knew the words and what was happening on the stage to such an

Panto can come as a shock to some tourists who believe they are simply going to see a straightforward musical play! But 'Oh no they're not!'

extent that the audience joined in and the barriers between those watching and those performing became fuzzily non-existent as the fourth wall seemed to crash around their ears.

# THE PANTOMIME MIX

Pantomime is a bit like a cake, get the mix wrong and it will fall flat. So exactly what goes into this mix to make a great Pantomime? What comes first? Now there's a debate all on its own, and to be honest it's a bit of a chicken and egg situation for each element is as important as the next and so for that reason alone we will look at the basic ingredients, as they say 'in no particular order', starting with 'The Art of Pantomime' quite simply for no reason what-so-ever!

# THE ART OF PANTOMIME

To start with let me point out to you that we rarely call Pantomime 'Pantomime', but instead affectionately refer to it by its shortened name of 'Panto'. From now on that is exactly what we will do here and I just hope that there is not lurking amongst you a reader with my bizarre insistence on enjoying a book – magazine or newspaper too for that matter – from the end to the beginning. Panto is confusing enough without adding to the confusion for goodness sake!

# AUDIENCE PARTICIPATION

*The audience participation tradition is said to have been 'invented' by that great audience clown, Joseph Grimaldi.*

'Audience Participation', these are the two words synonymous with Panto and the two words that best describe the 'art' of Panto. The curtain goes up on theatre, the show begins, the plot unfolds and the audience watch – well, that might be the case with most styles of theatre, but it has nothing at all to do with Panto. In Panto Land, the curtain goes up, the show begins and then it's anybody's guess what is going to happen next! Much depends on the audience participation sections, for remember they are unscripted; audience members were not a part of the rehearsal process and so can call out and say just what they want – and they do – often with hilarious results too. Audience participation is the beating heart of Panto as well as being the thread on which other gems hang, for throughout the performance the audience are urged to warn the goodies of an approaching baddie, asked to help find a missing object or to sing along with songs. The audience are a part of the cast; and because they are a part of the cast, they must of course have lines to say! Much to the amusement of overseas visitors who are perhaps experiencing Panto for the very first time it seems that everyone in the audience, except for themselves of course, not only know the lines, but know when to say them too, for it never varies from year to year, venue to venue or from one Panto to another for that matter, irrespective of the storyline. Examples are:

- 'He's behind you' – this is the call the audience are requested to shout out as a warning when some unwanted person makes an unwanted appearance
- 'Oh no it isn't' – 'Oh yes it is' – a bantering interchange between the audience and one or two of the cast members
- The Chase – when the chase involves the cast racing through the auditorium then of course the audience become involved; if the audience were made up of adults only, then they may be content to sit back and watch, but with an audience made up, in the greater part, of children then that's not an option. They want to be involved – in fact, they want to participate and can often be seen chasing some character or other around they auditorium – with the funniest part being that they seldom remember where their seat is when the chase is over! This means that Mum or Dad has to retrieve and reclaim their offspring, and so Mum and Dad join in too!
- The Song Sheet – take a song, ask the audience to join in and then invite small children onto the stage, without a prior rehearsal, to sing the song solo and you have audience participation of the most dangerous kind. Anything can happen and in fact usually does when you give a small child a microphone and make them the centre of attention
- 'Hiss … Boo' – this is what we all want to call out when someone we dislike enters our life, but good manners prevent us from doing so – well at least in the majority of cases – and so the opportunity to hiss and boo at the villain of the piece can be actually quite therapeutic

## STORYLINES

In general terms Panto is a fairy story where good triumphs over evil and the young man – who is really a young girl dressed as a young man – is the handsome son of a rather gregarious multi-coloured woman – who is really a man dressed as a woman – and falls in love with a beautiful young woman who is – wait for it – a woman! Love generally wins the day and the production usually finishes with a very lavish wedding scene. The storylines themselves generally have their roots in traditional fairy tales, often centuries old, and with a very simple and straightforward plot.

There are traditionally, and surprisingly, only a few Panto storylines. Although each year new ones emerge and call themselves a Panto, they are usually rejected by the audiences as 'Just Christmas stories and not proper Pantos'. It would seem, therefore, that part of the fun is to go along knowing exactly what you are going to see; the story is immaterial, it is the predictability of the content that matters and consists of tried and tested traditions which have been, and continue to be, passed down from one generation to the next. Any deviation from this traditional mix will almost certainly result in failure. In the past producers have been known to announce that they want to create a new and exciting form of Christmas Panto; some are even more daring and call their creation a 'Christmas Story'. This inevitably results in cries and moans from the children that 'It's not a proper Panto'. Suddenly, what is generally a child-friendly production has a decidedly unfriendly feel to it. The traditional and most popular Panto stories are given below.

| *Dick Whittington* | A poor young man and his cat beat the evil villain and he then becomes a wealthy young man and his cat; he marries the beautiful girl and is made Lord Mayor of London – three times. |
| --- | --- |
| *Puss in Boots* | Colin is left a cat in a will, which at first does not please him, and then, after he buys his cat some boots, he finds out that this is no ordinary cat, but is indeed a magical cat. Parents beware! Do not buy young children boots just after you have seen this Panto, but if you really must – then be sure to lock up the cat! |
| *Cinderella* | Cinderella is a poor young girl, who is treated badly by her Stepmother and her two Stepsisters and forced to live amongst the 'cinders'. Her Fairy Godmother then arranges for her to go to a |

ball where the Prince is looking for a wife – and guess what! Yes, he found her in the form of Cinderella.

*Snow White and the Seven Dwarfs*
This is another story in which a Wicked Stepmother plays a central role. Realising her Stepdaughter is more beautiful, the Wicked Stepmother arranges to have her killed, but of course it all goes wrong and Snow White lives, meets the Seven Dwarfs, survives another murder attempt and then is woken from a deep sleep by a kiss from a Prince.

*Aladdin*
Aladdin starts off as a lazy, good-for-nothing, young man and then into his possession comes not only a magic lamp, complete with its own Genie, but a magic ring – again complete with Genie! – and a magic flying carpet – sadly this time though, with no Genie attached. However, all in all it is no wonder that with all this help he beats the baddie, wins the girl and lives happily ever after.

*Jack and the Beanstalk*
A Giant is terrorising the land and the King offers the hand of his daughter in marriage to whoever slays said Giant. Jack sells the family's cow for magic beans which then grow into a beanstalk reaching up to the Giant's castle in the sky. He climbs the beanstalk, slays the Giant, hacks down the beanstalk and claims his bride.

*Sleeping Beauty*
The King and Queen have waited a long time for the birth of their beautiful daughter and so throw a lavish christening party. However, they forget to invite one particular fairy who, as a consequence, bestows not a gift but a curse upon the baby Princess; the curse being that at the age of 16 she will prick her finger and die. Another fairy comes to the rescue and although unable to overturn the curse, she does adapt it. So instead of dying when her finger is pricked, the Princess, will merely go

to sleep for a hundred years instead! After which time she will be woken by a kiss from a handsome Prince.

*Mother Goose* This is a Panto with a strong moral tale in which the Dame sacrifices her beloved Goose in pursuit of beauty. Realising her mistake she fights to win back her Goose.

Other stories, apparently sometimes 'masquerading' as pantos, are detailed below:

*Goldilocks and the Three Bears* A tale well known to everyone since childhood of a golden haired girl who comes across the home of three bears, each with their own proportionally sized belongings.

*Little Red Riding Hood* A young girl goes to visit her Grandmother, taking with her some goodies. However, when she arrives at her Grandmother's cottage it turns out that a wolf has eaten her and dressed himself up as the Grandmother in an attempt to fool the young girl. (For Panto purposes a circus theme is often incorporated into this particular story-line.)

*Peter Pan* The classic tale of a young boy called Peter Pan who never grew up and of how he and his fairy Tinker Bell visit the Darling children and take them to Neverland where they have numerous adventures. This tale is one which is becoming more and more accepted and looks as though it may well eventually cross over and be accepted as a traditional Panto.

*Babes in the Wood / Robin Hood* This is two productions 'mashed' or 'fused' into one – to use contemporary terminology – where two Babes are deserted in the forest by their Wicked Uncle's Henchmen. They are then predictably found by Robin Hood and Maid Marian who take them back to the safety of their

Each Christmas Pantos play in Britain from local village halls through to the large and impressive London Palladium.

| | |
|---|---|
| | encampment – the Wicked Uncle is, of course, the Sheriff of Nottingham! |
| *Robinson Crusoe* | Robinson Crusoe is shipwrecked on a desert island which appears not to be quite so lonely and deserted as in the original book as, for the sake of Panto fun, numerous characters turn up! |
| *Goody Two Shoes* | A poor orphan girl only had one shoe until a fairy cobbler made her not only a pair of shoes but a pair of magic shoes that changed her life for ever. |
| *Hop O' My Thumb* | Hop O' My Thumb was so tiny that he could do just that, 'hop onto a thumb'; he was the youngest of the seven stepsons of a poor woodcutter who was determined to rid himself of his cumbersome stepchildren. |

## AMATEUR OR PROFESSIONAL?

Should you go to see a professional production or an amateur production? Well, some people – and I'm afraid to say that this includes some of my own thespian, professional colleagues too – look down their noses at any production that isn't professional; this is not a point of view to which I personally subscribe. Generally, I say that any production which introduces Joe Public to the joys of theatre is a good production, and I don't care whether it is amateur or professional. I think we should just get – as we say – bums on seats and then worry about choices and standards.

## THEATRICAL NURSERY

Everything has a beginning and quite often within any learning environment at the beginning there is a nursery where the foundations are laid down and then built upon to achieve excellence – and Panto is no exception to this theory, though it is quite rightly disputed by some that Panto is not a theatrical nursery but is in fact a fully-fledged theatrical experience in its own right. There are, in my view, very strong arguments for both:

25

1. Theatrical nursery – it is indeed a theatrical nursery for just remember how many individuals were introduced to theatre through an annual trip to the local Panto. And how wonderful is that to enjoy theatre at the age of perhaps just 2 years, as indeed I was when I was taken to see my first Panto.

or

2. A fully-fledged theatrical experience – of course, it is that too; it is an art form in its own right after all and although, traditionally, rather a lot of making it up as you go along takes place – officially known by the cover term of ad libbing, this tradition is all a part of the Panto experience.

Every Christmas around the UK there are thousands of Pantos, amateur, professional, large scale, small scale, good and, shall we say, less good! For me though the important thing is that they are all pulling in the audiences, for a Panto is probably the only type of theatrical production that can almost guarantee a good audience. It is a part of the British way of life at Christmas; to buy a tree, put up the lights, eat turkey, mince pies and too much of everything else, invite relatives around that we rarely see and probably don't like, watch the Queen's speech and go to the Panto. If you are lucky enough to live near a big commercial theatre, then you will probably head off in that direction and delight in watching a well-known face from the TV strut their stuff on the boards, if not then you will probably wander down to your local village hall to watch your friends and neighbours aspire to theatrical heights.

We have talked a lot about Panto being full of traditions and so now let us take a look at some of those traditions.

## TRADITIONS AND SUPERSTITIONS

The world of theatre, as a whole, is a world steeped and shrouded in tradition and superstition. Many actions/events, etc. are traditionally always carried out or performed in a certain way, for no other reason than that it is quite simply tradition to do so. This, of course, makes thespians feel proud that they are a part of a profession that has its own regulations and rules; it is a bit like being a member of an exclusive club. As for superstitions, well there is no club quite like the thespian club on that point, for an actor's life is swathed in superstition – most know the fear surrounding the utterance of the name of that doomed 'Scottish Play', for example. And note that I shy far away from even typing the name, and as for typing the name of the Scottish King or the name of the Scottish King's wife – no way! Stupid I am not! So you see just how engrained it is in a thespian's way of life. As for Panto, well for every tradition and superstition in 'general' theatre, in Panto there are two! So let's just take a look a few of these.

- Traditionally, even in the 'normal world', we think of 'right' as being good and 'left' as being bad, which is probably why then in Panto the 'Good' Fairy traditionally always enters from stage right and the 'Bad' Demon King from stage left. (It is worth remembering here that right and left in theatre is from an actor's point of view and not from the point of view of the audience)
- When speaking it is tradition that the Panto Fairy always transfers her wand from her right hand to her left hand when encountering the evil Demon King; she does this to protect her heart from his evil wrath
- Some think that sweet throwing is a 'new' tradition in Pantos, but in fact it can actually be traced as far back as performances of the plays by Aristophanes, who incidentally was reputedly very annoyed by the practice!
- In the late nineteenth century it was usually the job of the Clown to throw the sweets (then called candies, of course) and nuts into the audience. Now they are usually thrown by the Dame or the Simple Simon character
- Audience participation extends to action songs too which for me is probably the greatest tradition of all. This involves a large screen – called a song sheet – being dropped onto the stage and displaying the words of a 'Panto Song'. (However, this wonderful tradition is now not carried out to the max, and sometimes sheets don't appear at all when current 'hit' songs are used; a sad sign of the times I'm afraid, and I think one that somewhat spoils the Panto, but then this is just a personal opinion. I much prefer to sing that old Panto classic 'There's a Worm at the Bottom of the Garden!') When the song sheet appears the audience then sing along, generally encouraged by the show's principal comedian. Once the audience is familiar with the song, which takes very little time as most

know the words anyway because they are either the traditional Panto songs or they are some current pop song, they are then very often divided into two parts, or even divided into stalls, dress circle, etc., after which ensues a singing competition when all are encouraged to out-sing each other – in volume of vocals rather than quality of vocals. The general atmosphere then becomes a little rowdy and excitable as everyone tries to out-sing everyone else. And this is before actions are added; yes I did say 'actions!' It goes like this:

Every member of the audience is then asked to repeat the song, whilst performing a series of actions. This in itself is extremely amusing as entire families are often expected to stand up and then sit down in quick succession, look under their seat, rub their tums, pat their heads, etc. 'Easy peasy', as they would say in Panto Land? Oh no it isn't! For entire family groups often consist of arthritic granny who can barely stand at all, let alone stand up and down several times in quick succession! Then there is Granddad who everyone, but he, knows is stone deaf but who insists on joining in the fun – generally one action behind everyone else, meaning that he is standing when the rest of the audience is sitting, etc., for, of course, not being able to hear the instructions he copies them! And as for the calling out all the responses as required, he insists on doing that too – but not quite as correctly as required. In fact, all eyes are often on Granddad wondering what on earth he is going to shout out next! As for going under the seat, surely that's just great fun; of course it is, but it has to be pointed out that many a child has in the past decided that staying there is even more fun, until his sister is sick over his protruding head, of course, an 'action' she performs whilst rubbing her tummy which is full of chocolate and ice cream; the 2-year-old of the family finds the head patting section so much funnier when he bangs (pats) his baby brother on the head, usually with some hard object. And what's mother doing whilst all of this is going on? Generally nothing for she can't move being hidden under a mound of discarded coats and bags so everyone else can join in the fun. Father meanwhile is proclaiming: 'I told you this was a bad idea!' A bad idea it might be – but it is traditional and what's more it will live on in the memories and hearts of those participating for ever more. I know, having progressed through the ranks from the child under the seat, through to the mother holding the coats and now the granny gingerly standing up and down! And I bet that after reading the above, you now recognise at what stage you are now!

Once the vocal sing off is over and the actions successfully executed, or not as the case may be, the grown-ups all sit back exhausted, whilst the next tradition takes over the theatre and that is the one where the children are encouraged – yes encouraged by the show's principal comedian – to go up onto the stage and sing the song, that has just worn out an entire audience, as a solo performance. Each night the comedian hopes for some precocious, pint-sized comic to step onto the boards, entertain the audience and so make his life much easier; and there is almost always one! This tradition, however, has a very practical reason behind its creation. You see, a long time ago it was decided that extra time was needed for the stage management team to prepare the set for the lavish walk-downs, which were growing each year to such an extent that they were almost productions in themselves. So these little child entertainers in their unpredictability could and can almost always be relied upon to buy that much-needed time for the backstage crew. Though one does have to feel sorry for the crew as no one can accurately predict just how much time they will have to change the scene as it varies with each performance and is reliant upon the child performers and just how much they are prepared to show off for that particular performance

- Another tradition governs the delivery of the last lines in the finale of a Panto which are traditionally written in rhyming couplets and, which tradition dictates, are never spoken in rehearsal but instead are spoken for the first time on opening night
- The 'walk-down' in theatre is traditionally taken according to importance within the cast and so the 'star' of the show is the last to take a bow, but not so in Panto Land where tradition dictates that the Principal Boy and Principal Girl walk down to take their bow *after* the star of the show
- The jokes in a Panto are often in the somewhat risqué, double entendre genre, the theory being it will entertain the adults whilst safely going over

the heads of the innocent children – thus keeping all of the audience happy and entertained

- There are even traditional jokes in Panto Land, jokes that are told year after year, jokes to which all Panto lovers know the punch line and yet jokes that continue to pull in the laughter. One of the oldest and best known jokes which actually refers to the opening of the Great Exhibition at Crystal Palace in 1851 is often still heard in even the most modern versions of *Cinderella*; it goes like this:

> 1st Ugly Sister: I will now get my foot into the crystal slipper.
> 2nd Ugly Sister: You couldn't get your foot into the Crystal Palace.

Another well-known popular joke found in *Cinderella* is:

> 1st Character: My teeth are like stars.
> 2nd Character: Yes they come out at night.

In *Sleeping Beauty* one can expect either the King or Queen, on hearing that they have been asleep for 100 years, to bring out the line: 'In that case I must go and put the cat out.' In the best sense of tradition, if audiences are not treated to their favourite joke then they have a feeling of being short-changed and so it is that these old chestnuts come out year after year after year. My personal favourite of them all is the question and answer routine which actually relies on delivery rather than a punch line:

> 1st Character: Why don't you grow up, stupid?
> 2nd Character: I have grown up stupid!

- Some superstitions are not the sole property of Panto Land, but in fact belong to the theatrical world as a whole, such as the belief that green is an unlucky colour to wear on the stage. Of course, this can be a huge problem if the Panto happens to be Robin Hood (not on the list of 'real' Pantos but sometimes performed as an addition or alternative). Add to this obvious colour problem the fact that at one time – and sometimes even now – ballet dancers would refuse to wear blue on the stage, unless wardrobe added some silver to the said costume, then things could get complicated for there is often an underwater ballet sequence in a Panto – in which, of course, blue is a rather necessary colour!

- Other superstitions which Pantomimists (have I just coined a new word for the purpose of this book?) share with thespians in general include not wanting to use real flowers on the stage in the belief that this will bring them bad luck. They don't object to the leading lady receiving a bouquet, though at the curtain call! However, receiving a bouquet of flowers at the stage door *before* a performance begins is considered to be a prediction of failure. Further superstitions include:

  - Not whistling on the stage for this is considered to be very unlucky. There is though a sensible and practical reason for this one. For it was that in the early days of theatre the flymen were often ex-sailors who were used to communicating with each other by a series of whistles. This meant that a whistle from a flyman could be the signal to another flyman to drop a 2-ton weight onto the stage. Now what could be more unlucky for an actor who was happily strolling and merrily whistling his way across the stage, if that weight were to drop onto his head – merely because he was whistling a little ditty

  - The dressing room is a minefield of problems for a superstitious actor/actress: to avoid bad luck then pictures must not be hung in the dressing room until after opening night; make-up boxes should never be cleaned out as this is said to bring bad luck; if an actress drops her comb the she must dance over it to avoid losing her job and if she drops her powder, then she must dance upon it to bring good luck; then there are the possible problems that could be created if more than one person washes his/her hands in the basin at the same time – do this and it is said that a quarrel will follow, but to avoid this then the pair involved should make the sign of the cross on the water; still in the dressing room, the actor/actress must remember not to leave behind his/her soap because that would mean their career would be over, well in that theatre anyway for the superstition states that they would never work in that particular theatre again

  - As well as all the usual hazards back stage such as cables, props, scenery, etc. an actor has to beware other actors – or indeed seek them out – for to be pinched before making a first entrance is said to bring good luck. And if you can't find someone to pinch you then make sure that you trip as you make your first entrance on the first night for that is a sign of success

The list of superstitions goes on and on and so you would think that to be an actor/actress you need all the luck in the world – but don't rely on another actor/actress wishing you good luck, for that would bring you bad luck! Best just to give up and hope for a bad dress rehearsal, because that is a good sign that the show will run smoothly.

# TRADITIONAL SCENES

This ingredient in the Panto mix is a part of the audience 'knowing what to expect' tradition and so of course it is imperative that these traditional scenes are included. Each Panto has its own scenes which must appear, such as the ballroom scene in Cinderella, for they are part of the plot, but other scenes are quite different for they are generally contrived for amusement only and actually have very little, if anything at all, to do with the actual plot. It is generally the comic characters who are involved in such scenes, which include:

• Slosh scene – this is the messy scene which can and should get out of hand. The children in the audience love it and the parents just pray that they won't try and re-enact it when they get home! Basically, this is a scene that involves anything that will make a mess, a big mess, such as the Wallpaper scene which involves a lot of messy wallpaper paste that inevitably goes everywhere and anywhere but on the wallpaper, a ladder with very dodgy and unpredictable rungs and of course a bucket that seems to have a life of its own; result, paste everywhere, no paper on the walls and a predictable heap of mess
• Schoolroom scene – here we have a scene with a long and traditional history, even pre-*commedia dell'art*e, in which one of the comic characters battles with a classroom full of naughty children
• Chase scene – this is a scene that often extends into the auditorium as characters chase one or more of the other characters around the Stalls

and even further afield, up into the Dress Circle, Upper Circle and even into the 'Posh Boxes'. Of course the children love it!

• Ghost scene – this is a scene that involves characters who, finding themselves alone in a scary place, also find themselves taunted by a ghostly figure, which they cannot see, but the audience can. This is of course another perfect excuse for the most well known of all the audience participation sequences – the calls of:

> 'He's behind you' –
> 'Oh no he isn't' –
> 'Oh yes he is!'

Interestingly, this series of calls has now even entered everyday vernacular

• Tree of Truth scene – one wonders whether the intention of this scene is to instil in children some sense of morality, to teach them that to tell a lie will result in something rather unpalatable happening to them? Well, to be absolutely honest who knows; maybe it is and maybe it isn't. Whatever the intention though the scene never loses its appeal and takes place when two of the comic characters – usually the Dame and the Simple Simon character – sit underneath some sort of tree and engage in a conversation that is not entirely truthful. Each time the Dame tells a lie, a piece of fruit falls on her head – or sometimes an article of her clothing mysteriously disappears, and it continues to happen over and over again, wherever she tells a lie, perhaps proving that those who lie will always be caught out. Sometimes these missiles are aimed at both characters and sometimes articles of clothing belonging to both characters mysteriously disappear too, the interpretation being entirely up to the writer and the director

## THE STOCK CHARACTERS OF PANTO LAND

Panto is somewhat different to all other theatrical productions in that each one, irrespective of the title and subject matter, has a set of stock characters who must be included – for they are included in *every* Panto; it's tradition and it is expected, only the name differs to help remind you which Panto you are actually watching. If just one of these characters is missing then there will be wails from the children – and adults too – that it is not a 'real' Panto! And you know what? It won't be a real Panto either, for the characters come before the storyline in this strange, wonderful and magical land.

This is what is so marvellous and delightful about Panto – the audience know the story, they know the characters; they know much of the dialogue too, including the 'happy ever after' outcome. It is all so comfortably predictable. Take this predictability out of the mix and the Panto simply won't work, to such an extent that it wouldn't even be a Panto; it would be just another theatrical performance – and that would never do. So, now let's get back to these stock characters and discover more about them; exactly who are these stock characters and what is their place and their role in the given Panto? Let's start with the character synonymous with the very word of Panto, and that is the Dame.

## DAME – 'A FELLER IN A FROCK'

The Dame in a Panto is generally a large, gregarious and out-going man who plays the part of a large, gregarious and out-going woman. *She* is usually the mother, nurse, aunt, etc. of one of the principal characters, or alternatively *she* could be the cook in a royal household or a schoolmistress in the village school. In fact, as long as she is there in some guise or other no one really cares, to be honest, who she is or where she fits – or doesn't fit for that matter – into the storyline! Her clothes are always over the top to the extent that they are actually quite ridiculous. Except in the Panto *Cinderella*, the Dame is always a 'goodie'; in *Cinderella*, she is a baddie, well to be more accurate 'they' are baddies, for there are actually two Dames in this Panto in the guise of the Ugly Sisters, (or 'The Uglies', as they are known in the business). Every successful actor who plays the part of Dame in Panto knows that the secret of his success is that it should be obvious that it is a man playing a part, for this is not a Drag act; the intention is not to be as womanly as possible, but to always be 'a feller in a frock'. Generally, she has a love interest in the Panto, which only adds to the comedy, of which she carries the largest part, and her romantic yearnings are often for the Simple Simon character of the piece – which also adds a little pathos, for he is clearly out of her reach. Oh how everyone loves the Panto Dame for she *is* Panto.

On to the Immortals; there is nothing real in a Panto and so the inclusion of Immortals is an obvious inclusion.

## THE IMMORTALS

The essential characters, of the Fairy Queen and Demon King, otherwise known as the Immortals, generally open a Panto with a rhyming prologue which explains the essence of the Panto in question. They are, unintentionally, humorous characters and are usually played straight but are traditionally funny – and usually corny into the bargain too, which leads to groans from the audience – another tradition! The Immortals are represented by the Good Fairy Queen and the Bad Demon King.

The Demon King is frequently greeted with hisses and boos, to the delight of the children who for some reason love the booing more than the cheering. Both tend to appear and disappear in puffs of smoke, which vary in effectiveness according to the size of the budget available, and sometimes according to whether or not the director decides to play this special effect for humour. But, for whatever reason, when the puffs fail this just adds to the hilarity of the situation, and no one 'traditionally' cares!

The next two characters are about as normal as one gets in Panto.

## THE PRINCIPAL BOY

Brave and of course handsome, the Principal Boy is often the title role as in *Jack and the Beanstalk* and *Aladdin*; if not, then he will probably be a Prince or a poor boy made good and he will of course be the star-crossed lover of the piece.

Historically and traditionally, this 'boy' role was always played by a girl, though in recent years this tradition has somewhat abated, which I do feel is a shame as it takes away some of the quirkiness for which Panto is famous. When the tradition is adhered to and the part is taken by a female then the most important characteristic feature necessary for a successfully played Principal Boy is a pair of 'long and stunning legs' which she/he usually and regularly slaps on the thigh in an exaggerated manner and at frequent intervals throughout the Panto – another quirky tradition which works well because when a female plays the part then she is always dressed in a short tunic to show off the legs. Bring back this tradition throughout Panto Land, I say, before it is lost altogether.

## THE PRINCIPAL GIRL

The Principal Girl can be a Princess or a poor and down-trodden servant girl, but one thing for sure is that she will always be very, very pretty, generally have a beautiful singing voice and be someone to whom all the little girls in the audience can look up to in awe and wonderment; every little girl should want to be the Principal Girl; if not then there is something amiss with the casting.

Sometimes it can seem like a bit of a non-part for an actress to play, for there is nothing really to get one's teeth into from an acting point of view, but for all those little girls, it is a vital and special role; especially in these days of the true and very real fairytale Princesses, such as Kate Middleton!

Another villain and that means more opportunity for hissing and booing.

## THE VILLAIN

Where there is good there is always bad, so as Panto is essentially about the good things in life it must have a baddie, and a villain is in fact necessary to heighten the qualities of the good guys – and it is, as I said, also an excuse for the audience to join in the game of more hissing and booing. (You may think this is funny, but beware sitting in front of someone whose false teeth are not a perfect fit when they are hissing and see how you feel about audience participation then!) These characters are always rather melodramatic, as in the old dramas – and the children love it. Adults on the other hand say they just pretend to love it, but we know better!

And then we have every child's friend in the guise of ...

## SIMPLE SIMON

This is the name given to the naïve goodie in Panto, though he is not simple and is rarely called Simon either! He is always the most lovable of all the characters and is generally the children's friend and frequently chats with the audience, usually involving them in the action by, for example, asking them to shout out a greeting to him each time he arrives on the stage, or perhaps by asking them to remind him to water a plant or some other such simple action. He can be actually any character at all but the most well known of the Simple Simon characters are Buttons in *Cinderella* and

Wishee Washee in *Aladdin* and, along with the Dame, he carries most of the comedy in the production. In fact, he is often the son of the Dame, though is sometimes even her love interest.

Panto is a fun experience and so comedy is absolutely essential to the mix and what better way than to start with the classic double act.

## THE DOUBLE ACT OR THE BROKERS MEN

This Double Act is actually the Double 'Comedy' Act in which one of the duo is generally the bright one and the other the dimwit. Otherwise known as the Brokers Men, they are usually the minor baddies working for the major Villain and bounce their comedy routines off each other as in the most traditional of double acts. In the Panto they often work alongside the other comedy parts of the Dame and the Simple Simon character. They are usually given ridiculous names such as: Lo and Hi.

In a performance where the costumes almost are parts in their own right it comes as no surprise then to know that some of the actors have to dress up as animals; their work – for the necessary CV – is called 'skins'.

## SKIN PARTS

Skin parts are where an actor dresses as an animal. This isn't actually a stock part, though usually a very welcome part, for what child wouldn't like to see an animal come to life; what adult wouldn't like it either! We all often imagine that we know what animals are thinking and this is the opportune moment to find out whether we are right. Although animals do not appear in every Panto, when they do they are much loved by the audience and are most definitely an integral part of the whole. Pantos in which animals always appear are of course *Dick Whittington*, *Aladdin*, *Puss in Boots*, *Mother Goose*, *Goldilocks and the Three Bears*, *Little Red Riding Hood*, *Cinderella* and *Jack and the Beanstalk*. Where an animal is neither needed nor required, then quite often the good old favourite – the Panto horse – is introduced, or any other animal an enterprisingly artistic director can weave into the plot too. To the non-professional these seem very easy roles to play, but try telling that to an actor who has been rehearsing a tap-dancing routine for weeks on end as the back end of a cow! Skin work is a specialist skill, especially when the animal concerned has four legs.

Now let us identify characters in the most popular Pantos by their names, some of whom are stock characters and some of whom are peculiar to the given Panto. Then there are those who are just downright essential, I mean imagine a Panto without the dancing villagers, and as for the Babes, well that's where many dreams start. The older chorus dancers are often third year students taken from some of the finest performing art colleges in the country, all gaining experience before graduation, and the younger dancers – known as 'Babes' – are generally taken from a local dance school. Most little girls' – and even some little boys' – greatest wish for Christmas is to appear in the local Panto 'at the big theatre' and most local dance schools want to be the provider for that raises their status in the community, increases their number of pupils and thus their annual income – yes Panto is big business for all concerned.

## OTHER CHARACTERS

| Character | Description |
| --- | --- |
| Chorus (Adult Dancers, the Babes) | The essential all-singing, all-dancing chorus. |
| Abanazar | A character in *Aladdin*, he is the wicked sorcerer who attempts to steal the magic lamp from Aladdin. |
| Aladdin | The Principal Boy in *Aladdin*, he is the lazy son of a washer woman who eventually makes his fortune with the help of a magic lamp. |
| Alderman Fitzwarren | Father of Alice and employer of Dick in *Dick Whittington*. |
| Alice Fitzwarren | The love interest for Dick in *Dick Whittington*. |
| Badroubaldour, Lady | The Emperor of China's Daughter in *Aladdin* and the young woman with whom Aladdin falls in love. |
| Baron Hardup | This is Cinderella's father in *Cinderella*. He is under the control of his second wife and her two daughters – known as the Ugly Sisters. |

Baroness Hardup  Cinderella's Wicked Stepmother.

Billy  Sometimes called Silly Billy, this is the name given to Mother Goose's son in the Panto *Mother Goose.*

Blunderbore  The name of the Giant in *Jack and the Beanstalk.*

Brokers Men  These are the two comic characters who are often played by a well-known double act of the day and are generally the two comic bailiffs in the Panto *Cinderella.* Recently, they have also become established characters in several other Pantos such as *Mother Goose.*

Buttercup  The name sometimes given to the cow in *Jack and the Beanstalk.*

Buttons  Cinderella's faithful friend in the Panto *Cinderella.* He was the creation of the Panto writer H.J. Byron.

Camel  Needless to say, a skinned part, the camel often appears in *Aladdin.*

Captain and Mate  The two comedians on Alderman Fitzwarren's ship the *Saucy Sally* in *Dick Whittington.* The names of these characters change from Panto to Panto and the writers often call upon current trends to name them.

Chinese Policemen  The chase scene is a traditional scene of Panto and in *Aladdin* it is the Chinese policemen who do the chasing.

Cinderella  Principal Girl and title role in the Panto of the same name who finds herself ill-treated and reduced to a scullery maid by the woman her widower father has married and so who is now her Stepmother.

Colin  This is usually – though not exclusively – the name given to the Principal Boy in *Puss in Boots* and *Mother Goose.*

Daisy  The name usually given to the cow in *Jack and the Beanstalk.*

Dame Durden  One of the names given to the Dame in *Jack and the Beanstalk.*

39

| | |
|---|---|
| Dame Trott | One of the alternative names given to the Dame in *Jack and the Beanstalk*. |
| Dandini | This is one of the most famous of Panto names – and the one that most, and even the youngest, of children know. It is the name given to he who is the valet to Prince Charming in *Cinderella*. |
| Dame | A role played by a man as long ago as 1731, it has long been a male stronghold and probably the best loved of all characters in Panto. The character itself is the comic (lead) female character and is often the hero's mother. The names vary according to the Panto. |
| Dwarfs | Of which there are seven in the Panto *Snow White and the Seven Dwarfs*. |
| Dick Whittington | The title role and hero of the Panto *Dick Whittington*. |
| Demon King | The Demon King is one of the Immortals and probably the most evil of the baddie characters who make their appearance in Pantos. His entrances are usually made in a green light stage left, from where he threatens the cast and audience alike. |
| Fairy Godmother or Good Fairy | Fairy Godmothers or Good Fairies appear in Pantos just to make sure everything goes to plan and everyone lives happily ever after. Sometimes they don't have a name and other times they may be given a name. |
| Fairy Bowbells | The name often attributed to the Good Fairy in *Dick Whittington*. |
| Fairy Tulip | The name sometimes given to the Good Fairy in *Jack and the Beanstalk*. If the name is not Tulip then it is generally something connected to a garden, such as Daffodil, Rose, Crocus – but not Shed, Fairy Shed might be connected to the garden but somehow doesn't have the same ring about it! |
| Fleshcreep | The traditional name given to the Giant's Henchman in *Jack and the Beanstalk*. |

| | |
|---|---|
| Genie | A supernatural being who appears primarily as the Genie of the Lamp – and the ring – in *Aladdin*. |
| Henchman | Usually a Huntsman or Woodman who is sent into the forest to 'dispose of' Snow White in *Snow White and the Seven Dwarfs*. |
| Idle Jack | The Hero's best friend and sidekick in *Dick Whittington*. |
| Immortals | These are the supernatural characters and include both baddies and goodies who each in their turn influence the plot. Such characters generally speak in rhyming couplets. |
| Jack | The hero in *Jack and the Beanstalk* who, although a warm-hearted individual, is a lazy boy as well as being unscrupulous and sharp-witted. |
| Jill | Traditionally the name given to the Principal Girl in *Mother Goose* and sometimes it is also the name given to the Principal Girl in *Jack and the Beanstalk*. |
| King Gander | The Goose King – and sometimes called just that – in *Mother Goose*. |
| King Rat | The name of the Baddie in *Dick Whittington*. |
| Muddles | Generally the name given to the Simple Simon character in *Snow White*. |
| Prince Charming | The Prince who wins the love of *Cinderella* in the Panto of the same name. |
| Prince(s) | Handsome Princes litter the world of Fairy Tales and Panto Land alike and frequently their names vary from one Panto to another, often on the whim of a writer; sometimes, however, they are just called 'Prince', with no other name added. |
| Princess(s) | Like the handsome Princes, beautiful Princesses also feature regularly in Fairy Tales and Panto Land alike and often their names too vary from one Panto to another, and again often according to the writer's whim; and yet |

again they too are sometimes just called 'Princess' without the addition of another name.

Prince Florimond Following Charles Perrault's lead in his original story of Sleeping Beauty, this, or a variation on it, is traditionally and usually the name given to the Prince in *Sleeping Beauty*.

Princess Aurora In Charles Perrault's original story of Sleeping Beauty the Princess is called Aurora, and so once more many producers of Pantos have followed his lead, making this the traditional name for the Princess in *Sleeping Beauty* the Panto, though some predictably go for the name Beauty!

Sarah the Cook Usually the name given to the Dame character in *Dick Whittington*.

Simple Simon Simple Simon is primarily a nursery rhyme character who has crossed over into Panto Land. In *Jack and the Beanstalk* he often pops up as Jack's brother and, when he does, in this Panto he is actually just called Simon, although in some other Pantos he has another name such as Buttons in Cinderella. He is portrayed as a comical and somewhat dim-witted fellow and often appears as the best friend or brother of the Principal Boy.

Snow White The heroine and title role of the Panto by the same name; contrary to her name, the part is always played by an actress with jet-black hair.

Squire The Squire appears in *Jack and the Beanstalk*, though the full name varies from Panto to Panto.

Tinker Bell This is the name given to the Fairy in J.M. Barrie's *Peter Pan* but in Panto World the part of Tinker Bell is often dehumanised and played by a point of light, which darts feverishly around the stage and some producers/ directors have more recently favoured their Tinker Bell on roller skates. This Christmas 'entertainment' is now becoming increasingly popular as a Panto and many say is on the cusp of being accepted into the exclusive Panto club.

| | |
|---|---|
| Tommy | The name always given to the cat in *Dick Whittington*. |
| Ugly Sisters | Known in Panto Land as the Uglies, they are the vain and cruel Stepsisters of Cinderella. Generally, one of the sisters is tall, thin and arrogant, whilst the other is frequently short, fat and a little slow on the uptake. They are always a 'double act' in the Panto, if not in their general entertainment life. |
| Vegetable Fairy | This character, although now a standard and accepted Panto character, is a relatively recent addition to the Panto *Jack and the Beanstalk* and frequently goes by the name Sweetcorn. |
| Widow Twankey | Aladdin's mother who appears in *Aladdin* and who is one of the best loved of all Panto Dames. |
| Wishee Washee | He is the Simple Simon character in the Panto *Aladdin* and is the loyal and incompetent laundry assistant to Widow Twankey. |

## COMEDY – OR 'THE FUNNY BITS'

All Pantos must have a good smattering of humour; of course, there are the comedic characters and the comedy scenes too, but what about the jokes? Well, audiences expect to hear topical jokes – i.e., jokes about politicians and other famous people, jokes about current topics or anything that is a part of everyday life, and especially 'local' jokes about the town, or community, in which the Panto is currently playing. So writers certainly have their research work cut out. Then there are what some would say 'the smutty' jokes, for traditional Panto has a parallel script for the adults, a script that is full of innuendo and thankfully one that goes over the heads of the excited youngsters or even the naive and innocent adults for that matter. Add to this an over the top and very messy slapstick scene where everyone really does get *very* messy and often very wet too, and yes that includes the audience – well at least those stupid enough to sit on the first

43

two rows – and you will laugh 'til you cry, as you will at the ridiculous costumes and the all-singing, all-dancing animals. Talking animals bring out a mixture of the 'Aww' factor and laughter, sometimes both and it is not so much as what they say, as the way they say it, or do it. I mean it is not every day one sees a tap-dancing cow walking down the street, is it, or a camel in a tutu for that matter, but in Panto it almost seems normal and is certainly accepted as a part of the events/storyline which, let's be honest, is hilarious in itself.

Now, any of my students will tell you that my favourite saying is 'Theatre is a visual art'. In other words, if it doesn't look right then the chances are it won't be right. For you see the sense of sight has a great influence on all the other senses, to the point at times of overriding what we can hear, touch, smell and taste. As just one example, think about this. Imagine that you have been told to listen to a piece of music in order to identify a particular section – for whatever reason. Do you know what most of you will do? You will close your eyes; you will close your eyes because what you see has such an influence upon what you are trying to listen to, that you just have to cut out that sense. Okay, one more example. You are tasting a new piece of chocolate which you have been assured is the best ever and tastes like pure silk. What do you do? That's right, you've got it. You close your eyes again, this time in order to savour the full impact of the taste. Much as I would love to, I am sure that I don't have to go into more detail by giving more examples! What I am trying to say is what you see is SO important and can change a generally dull scene into a comedic scene. It's quite simple really, the way a Panto looks – and by that I mean costumes, scenery, sets, etc. – plays a great part in the overall perception and enjoyment of the piece, and never more so than in the comedy sections, of which of course there are many in a Panto. We want to be amused and laugh at what we see before even one single word is uttered, or a single action/piece of business is played out.

Identifying the funny bits … Having established then that anything comedic must 'look' funny to be truly effective, then let us set about identifying the comic elements within a Panto, beginning first with the characters.

## THE DAME

Why is she funny? Well, to start with, 'she' is a 'he', and is outrageous in the extreme. Her costumes are generally downright silly and her behaviour ludicrous. She looks anything but 'real' and therefore everything we see on, and about her, makes the audience laugh. Her character is an ever constant presence and is woven throughout the plot in all Pantos – this means that she is on and off the stage for at least 2 hours and so has the added advantage that she gets to wear more and more of her ridiculous costumes, thus enhancing her comedic appearance.

## SIMPLE SIMON

Not as outrageously funny in appearance as the Dame, he tends to look more pathetic evoking the 'Aww' factor from the audience and a few slaps around the head from the Dame – which is always funny!

## THE DOUBLE ACT

These two characters' clothes are quite often ill-fitting and so used to achieve the visual effect. Personally, I always feel sorry for the straight guy as he sets up the gags and yet it is the more obvious comedian that everyone loves!

## THE IMMORTALS

Played straight, these guys can be really funny in their sarcastic delivery of comedic lines which are generally more appreciated by the adults in the audience. A considerable amount of smoke/dry ice tends to accompany the appearance of this pair of characters and when this strays into the audience, either by design or by accident, the youngsters always find it hilarious.

## THE BADDIES

The baddies are often played for comedic effect and can be very funny in their ineptitude, which of course makes them less frightening for the younger members of the audience; visually they will frequently have 'equipment' which doesn't work or isn't real, such as guns which, when fired, merely drop down a flag displaying the word 'bang' rather than emitting a bullet! Such an action is always accompanied by roars of laughter from the children, again proving the power of the visual effect.

## COMEDIC SCENES

Then, of course, there are the scenes which have been created with the sole purpose of making the audience laugh. There are those that are set up to make as much mess or create as much mayhem as possible – especially when that mess and mayhem overspill into the audience. Other parts which are also an active part of the Panto comedy mix include props that don't work, costumes that fall to bits and scenery that moves or appears to have a mind and personality of its own, once more proving that theatre is a visual art and never more so than when the 'funny bits' are involved. And, of course, we mustn't forget the superbly crafted dialogue, courtesy of the writer, which includes the predictable lines, predictable exchanges and of course the predicable corny jokes – a lot of hard work goes into creating a mess and making people laugh!

*Chapter 2*

# ONCE UPON A TIME –
# PANTOMIME STORY LINES

O*nce upon a time…* there was a story, usually with a moral, which was taken, adapted, changed, embellished and so on to make it enjoyable and palatable to all; this story was then played out annually – around Christmas time – upon a stage to excited audiences, and guess what? The audience were even asked to join in at times! Everyone knew the story; everyone knew the ending where all the good guys lived happily ever after and the bad guys got their just deserts – oh, if only real life were like that! And yet despite everyone knowing the story so well, Charles Perrault's audiences returned year after year to watch again. Parents took their children and then when those children grew up, they in turn took their own children, and so it went on down the years and generations, proving once and for all that 'familiarity *does* not breed contempt' after all.

This story is what we all know as a Panto, and each year is played before thousands and thousands of theatre-goers across the UK. Although the stories remain essentially the same, there are slight variations and so no two *Dick Whittington* Pantos for example will be identical; okay, so Dick will always have a cat and he will always marry Alice Fitzwarren, but there may be other slight variations, which only adds to the fun, I suppose, and introduces just a little unpredictability to the much-loved predictability – bizarre! And so here we have what to expect in your favourite Panto.

## *CINDERELLA* THE PANTO

### ORIGINS

Taking 'Cinderella' as the theme of good triumphing over evil rather than as a story, then its origins can be traced way back in time for there are many tales of the oppressed emerging as the victor. But the story of Cinderella as we know it today is actually taken from the seventeenth-century writings of Charles Perrault.

## FIRST PRODUCTION

The first production of *Cinderella* was at the Theatre Royal, Drury Lane in 1804.

## CHARACTERS INCLUDE

| | |
|---|---|
| Baron Hardup | This is the name now generally given to the role of Cinderella's father, although other names can and are used, such as Baron Stoneybroke. |
| Baroness | The Baroness is Cinderella's wicked Stepmother. |
| Brokers Men | There are usually two of them and throughout the Panto they chase the Baron for money giving the opportunity for numerous chase and slapstick scenes. |
| Buttons | The lovable comic who usually has feelings for Cinderella, though she treats him as her brother. Interestingly, his costume is usually red or blue with a lot of buttons – much like a bell boy would wear. It is Buttons who talks to and has a relationship with the audience – he is the Simple Simon character in this particular Panto. |
| Cinderella | The title role of *Cinderella* is generally played by a pretty and waif-like girl; her name is often shortened to Cinders. |
| Dandini | Dandini is Valet to the Prince (Charming), and in some Panto scripts he is involved in a scene of mistaken identity where the Ugly Sisters make a play for him – believing him to be the Prince; though how this could happen is a mystery as tradition says that the part of the male Dandini be played by a female with long and |

beautiful legs, but then the Ugly Sisters are generally butch men in female clothes – so confusing but who cares!

Fairy Godmother    She is the one who through her magic creates all of the necessary trappings in order that Cinders 'May go to the ball'.

Prince    The Prince is the love interest for Cinderella and is generally called Prince Charming.

Ugly Sisters    This comic pair of sisters, known in the business as the Uglies, sometimes replace the part of the Dame in this particular Panto.

## THE PANTO STORYLINE OF *CINDERELLA*

*Once upon a time* ... a widower, who was the father of a young, mild-mannered and sweet-tempered daughter, married his second wife who was, in turn, the mother of two daughters too. This woman was thoroughly despicable and controlling, traits which she passed on to her two daughters, who incidentally usually have ridiculous names, but are actually known to the audience as the Ugly Sisters, Sadly, this mix of temperaments did not make for a happy household though, and so it was that the Stepmother and her two daughters made the younger girl do all of the housework. When she had finished the housework she was then made to sit in the scullery amidst the cinders – hence the name Cinderella. Living in this unhappy household could also be found a manservant by the name of Buttons. He is in love with Cinderella, but lacks the

49

courage to tell her and is the character who primarily interacts with the audience.

On one particular day it came to pass that the Prince of the land invited all the young ladies in his Kingdom to a ball; he did this solely because he felt it would enable him to choose a wife. However, Cinderella's two Stepsisters were invited, but she was not. Although she helped the pair to prepare for the ball, she was naturally very upset at being left out and on the night in question sobbed alone in the scullery after they had left.

It was at this point that Cinderella's Fairy Godmother dutifully appeared and promised to help her get to the ball. Of course, though, Cinderella had none of the necessary trappings to take her to such an event, but fortunately the Fairy Godmother was able to use her magic to 'make things happen'. So it was that she then set about turning a pumpkin into a coach, mice into horses, a rat into a coachman and some lizards into the necessary footmen. Of course, this was all very well but Cinders was still dressed in rags, but not for long, for the Fairy Godmother then set about changing Cinderella's rags into a beautiful ball gown, complete with an exquisite pair of glass slippers. Cinderella was now set and all ready for the ball – except for just one minor detail.

It was at this point that Cinderella's Fairy Godmother broke the news to her that the magic spells she had woven would all be broken on the stroke of midnight and it would be then that the coach would be no more than a vegetable once again and the horses and the coachman vermin, whilst the footmen would revert to being lizards. But worst news of all was that Cinderella herself would be stripped of all her finery and would once more be dressed just in her rags. The only way, she was told, to avoid all of this humiliation was to be sure to leave the ball and be safe back home amongst the cinders before the final stroke of midnight had sounded.

At the ball everyone was overawed by the beauty of the mysterious stranger – who the audience knew to be Cinderella; not even her Stepsisters recognised her and as for the Prince, well he was totally smitten with her and so was shocked when, having lost all track of time and in somewhat of a panic, she suddenly left the ball – and indeed him too – just before the clock struck midnight. It was at this point though that in her haste she lost her glass slipper on the steps of the Palace when she was running away, and so when the Prince chased after her he was able to retrieve and use it in his search for her. And so it was that he and his manservant, Dandini, searched the land for the beautiful woman who may have lost her slipper, but had stolen his heart.

When the Prince and his entourage arrived at Cinderella's home it was her two Stepsisters who appeared first, to try on the glass slipper, but of course it didn't fit them and it was only when the Prince asked if there was anyone else in the house that Cinderella appeared. The glass slipper fitted her perfectly and she was able to produce the matching other slipper which had also stayed intact, despite the powerful spell.

Cinderella then married her Prince and even forgave her two Stepsisters and so ... *everyone lived happily ever after.*

Is it a boy; is it a girl? Who cares it's a Panto.

## AND FINALLY

*Cinderella* is reputedly the most popular of all the Pantos, although preferences do change as decades pass

- And who can answer this question: Why and how did the slippers stay intact when everything else didn't?

## *SNOW WHITE AND THE SEVEN DWARFS* THE PANTO

### ORIGINS

Snow White and the Seven Dwarfs comes from a collection of folk tales which were written and collected by the Grimm Brothers, Jacob and Wilhelm Grimm – their surnames are usually reversed though, as they actually came to be known as 'The Brothers Grimm'. The tales were published in the early 1800s. In 1823 these tales were translated from the brothers' native language of German and published in English for us to enjoy too.

## FIRST PRODUCTION

Interestingly, the first *Snow White* Panto actually came after Walt Disney's film version of the story of Snow White, for it would appear that it was he who in fact recreated an interest in this folk tale, which had in fact been around for over 200 years.

## CHARACTERS INCLUDE

| | |
|---|---|
| Snow White | This obviously is the title role and is usually played by a young and beautiful girl, with jet-black hair. |
| Prince | In the original tale this particular Prince did not have a name, so giving a free rein to the producers and/or writers to call him whatever they wished or, as is more often the case, to simply call him the Prince. As he has to kiss Sleeping Beauty then the part usually defies tradition and is played by a man. |
| Wicked Queen | Another character which the Brothers Grimm failed to name and so one that is often just called 'The Wicked Queen' – in case no one has noticed. |
| Dame | This is a difficult one for there is no precedent for the part of the Dame here; there isn't a named Dame and in fact in many productions there isn't one at all, though some do add one as a Nurse to the Princess in the belief that a Panto isn't a Panto without a Dame – and oh no, it isn't. |
| Muddles | This is the name given to the comic/Simple Simon character. |
| Seven Dwarfs | Rather self-explanatory! |
| Henchman | Usually a Huntsman or Woodman who is sent into the forest to 'dispose of' Snow White. |

# THE PANTO STORYLINE OF SNOW WHITE AND THE SEVEN DWARFS

*Once upon a time* ... in a far off land – somewhere – there lived a Wicked Queen, obsessed by what she believed to be her unrivalled beauty. The Panto frequently opens with the Wicked Queen uttering into a mirror the immortal words: 'Magic Mirror on the wall, who is the Fairest one of all?' To which every child knows the answer is Snow White and so shout out to this effect. The mirror, however, proclaims the Wicked Queen as the fairest of all – but not for long, eh! So this over, we have immediately established the good and the bad of the Panto and the production proper can begin.

It is Snow White's birthday and a party is to be held for her. It is at this party that the Prince first sees Snow White and falls in love with her – it clearly being love at first sight for him. She now has everything, looks and the love of a handsome Prince too. The Wicked Queen hates her; she hates her even more though when once again the mirror is consulted as to who is the fairest of all and on this occasion answers Snow White! This seals the hatred of the Wicked Queen and she orders Snow White to be killed.

A Huntsman is despatched into the forest to kill Snow White; he is told to return with the heart of the poor, unsuspecting girl. However, he fails in his task and takes back the heart of a pig instead, hoping to fool the Wicked Queen. In the meantime, Snow White has run off deeper into the forest where she stumbles across a quaint little cottage, where everything appears to be in multiples of seven. It is the home of the Seven Dwarfs.

Snow White could quite happily have lived *happily ever after* at this point in the story, but it was not to be. The Wicked Queen, realising that Snow White had not been killed as she ordered but was still alive and well, living with the Seven Dwarfs deep in the forest, was determined to seek her out and complete the job herself. And so it was that this evil woman, dressed as an old hag, appeared on the doorstep of the cottage where she persuaded Snow White to take a bite out of a poisoned apple before running away. The Wicked Queen wrongly believed that she had finally killed Snow White, but she had actually only fallen into a deep sleep. Her seven little friends were distraught when they discovered their new friend in a deep, deep sleep from which they couldn't wake her. But they were distraught only until the arrival of the Prince whose magical kiss broke the spell and brought the Princess back to life. The fate of the Wicked Queen in each production of this Panto depends very much upon the creativity of the writer; once that is sorted then, of course … *everyone lives happily ever after.*

## AND FINALLY

- Have you ever wondered why there are seven dwarfs and not six or eight? Well, it is quite simple really because it would seem that the number seven has long since been considered as a lucky number – just look at the evidence

There are the Seven Wonders of the Ancient World:

1. Great Pyramid of Giza – an Egyptian tomb
2. Hanging Gardens of Babylon – multi-levelled gardens with water features
3. Statue of Zeus at Olympia – statue of the Greek God in a purpose-built temple
4. Temple of Artemis – a temple that took over 100 years to construct
5. Mausoleum of Halicarnassus – broken-hearted Artemisia built this tomb for her dead husband Mausolus, who, in line with ancient tradition, also just happened to be her brother
6. Colossus of Rhodes – a giant statue of the Greek god Helios
7. Lighthouse of Alexandria – built circa 280 BC and which for many centuries was one of the tallest structures in the world

And then you have to remember:

It took seven days to create the world – which is lucky for us, for without that there would be no human race – and so no Pantos

- All of the Jewish feasts last for seven days
- The charmed family member is reputedly the seventh son of the seventh son
- It was Shakespeare who told us of the seven ages of man, which are, of course, infant, student, lover, soldier, justice, maturity and senility
- There are seven sisters (stars) in the night sky
- And so finally we have the Seven Dwarfs in the tale of Snow White

Recently children have been playing the part of the dwarfs in *Snow White and the Seven Dwarfs* – wearing funny heads!

Sometimes the lack of availability of 'actor' dwarfs around the Christmas period will prevent a producer using *Snow White* as his/her chosen Panto. Though more recently children have been used wearing cartoon comedy heads. Thanks to the Disney film, everyone is familiar with the names of the Seven Dwarfs, but not everyone realises that when they go to see *Snow White and the Seven Dwarfs* Panto then the names will be different to the ones they know. The reason for this is because the names used in the film are the sole copyright of Walt Disney.

## *ALADDIN* THE PANTOMIME

### ORIGINS

The Panto *Aladdin* has its origins in the *The Tales of a Thousand and One Arabian Nights,* or often more simply known by its shortened title of *Arabian Nights.* In the *Arabian Nights* Scheherazade tells these tales to her husband the King, wins time and eventually her life. The King, you see, it seems is set on revenge after his first wife was unfaithful to him and so he decided to marry a different woman each and every day, and then execute his new bride on the following morning – not very romantic! But his new and final wife, Scheherazade, had other ideas and so, determined to stay alive for as long as possible, and certainly longer than the previous wives, each night told her husband an exciting story with promises that she would finish it the next day: 1001 nights later, her plan worked and her life was saved.

# FIRST PRODUCTION

Although there were earlier productions of *Aladdin*, the first true production of the Panto was at the Strand Theatre in 1861.

## CHARACTERS INCLUDE

Abanazar       The Villain, or the Baddie, of the Panto.

Aladdin       Aladdin is the traditional Panto Principal Boy, often played by a girl but equally a role open to and played by young boys.

Chinese Policemen    The chase scene is a traditionally expected part of every Panto and those expectations are generally fulfilled in Aladdin by the Chinese Policemen.

Princess       The Princess is the love interest and over time has been known by many names, although now the children are disappointed when, thanks to the

*Aladdin* is visually the most spectacular of all the Pantos.

influence of the popular Disney film, she is not called Princes Jasmine and so for that reason more and more producers are giving in to 'popular demand' and the Princess is called Princess Jasmine. This leads us, though, to the more intelligent child who will invariably ask the question: 'If Mr Disney lets the Panto people use the name Jasmine, then why won't he let them use the names of the Dwarfs?' And they have a point there, don't they?

Widow Twankey     This part is the Dame of the Panto; she is Aladdin's mother and the widow of a tailor.

Wishee Washee     Wishee Washee is the Simple Simon character of this Panto; sometimes it is played by a double comedy act, in which case the part is then called Wishee *and* Washee.

## THE PANTO STORYLINE OF *ALADDIN*

*Once upon a time* … there lived a young, and some might say lazy, young man called Aladdin. Now, Aladdin was the good for nothing son of Widow Twankey and they lived together in Old Peking.

The Panto *Aladdin* generally begins with a prologue during which we meet the Baddie Abanazar when we see him summoning the Genie of the Ring. It is this Genie who reveals to Abanazar that in the far off land of China there lives a boy called Aladdin. He tells Abanazar that only Aladdin can provide him with the magic lamp he so desires. On this news Abanazar commands the Genie of the Ring to transport him to China where the Panto proper then begins.

Meanwhile, in China, Aladdin has defied the orders of the ruling Vizer and has gazed upon his beautiful daughter Jasmine – or whatever name she is called in the Panto in question – and as a consequence he has fallen madly in love with her. This is not good because the Vizer has decreed that anyone caught gazing at his daughter will be executed! Abanazar arrives in China courtesy of his own personal Genie and he visits Aladdin where he is under guard, passing himself off as the brother of his father – and so Aladdin's long, lost uncle! Aladdin thinks he will be his saviour, and although Abanazer manages to spirit him away from his captors, he is of course anything but a saviour as Aladdin is about to find out when he is locked away in the Cave of Jewels.

The magic lamp Abanazar is desperate to own is in this Cave of Jewels and so he instructs Aladdin to find it for him, but Aladdin is more interested in acquiring the numerous jewels for himself and refuses to find the lamp for Abanazar, who then loses his temper and locks him in the cave. Aladdin, though, is wearing a magic ring with its own personal Genie – yes, another Genie – who helps him to escape from the cave, complete with the magic lamp which includes that Genie, of course!

*Aladdin* – not the Panto for the superstitious theatre-goer; or so they say!

All would seem well as Aladdin soon wins the love of the Princess; and the Genie of the Lamp builds him and his bride to be a huge palace. However, the Princess is unaware of the magic properties the lamp holds and when a pedlar arrives – the evil Abanazar in disguise – selling new lamps for old, she hands over the 'old' magic lamp in exchange for a bright, new, shiny one! Abanazar then commands the Genie of the Lamp to spirit away the palace with the Princess still inside.

Aladdin arrives home to find not only his bride to be missing, but his home too. Imagine it, you come home from an ordinary day at the office and not only has your family disappeared but so has your house too! But he, of course, still has the ring and so *that* Genie arranges for Aladdin to set off in hot pursuit, courtesy of a magic flying carpet! Of course he finds his Princess, retrieves the lamp and transports everyone back to China. Aladdin thinks up some fate worse than death for Abanazar – which varies with each Panto – and then of course ... *everyone lives happily ever after.*

## AND FINALLY

- *Aladdin* may be considered the most spectacular, of all the Pantos, thanks to its oriental backdrop, but in the world of theatre it is also considered to be the 'unlucky' Panto just as Shakespeare's Scottish Play is seen as the play which will inevitably bring back luck to all associated with the production. Then there is Arthur Miller's *The Crucible*, which is thought to bring bad luck; the reason for this apparently being the associated themes of magic. So, although magic might be exciting, some fervently believe that it can also be very unlucky. Probably best then not encourage your children to become magicians!

# *DICK WITTINGTON* THE PANTOMIME

## ORIGINS

This is a Panto that is actually based on a true story – though, of course, embellished somewhat when used as the basis for a Panto plot. There actually did exist a 'real' Richard Whittington, who in the late fourteenth and early fifteenth century did also become Lord Mayor of London.

The real Richard Whittington was born in the mid-fourteenth century as the son of a Gloucestershire knight. He was not a poor man, as in the Panto, but a man of great wealth who opened a mercer's shop in London. He was a friend of royalty and indeed loaned money to the royals of the time and eventually bequeathed his amassed fortune to charitable and public purposes.

## FIRST PRODUCTION

The first recorded production of *Dick Whittington* was in 1814, and it was in this particular production that the great Panto clown Joseph Grimaldi played the Dame, Cecily Suet.

## CHARACTERS INCLUDE

| | |
|---|---|
| Dick Whittington | Dick Whittington, as one would expect, is the hero of the piece. |
| Tommy the Cat | The Cat in this Panto is always called Tommy, or should be anyway, and is always a male cat and usually played by a very agile and acrobatic dancer. |

The Cat is, of course, a great favourite with the children in the audience.

**Alice Fitzwarren** — The Principal Girl and love interest of Dick Whittington, she was responsible for finding Dick work in her father's store.

**Alderman Fitzwarren** — Alice's father and employer of Dick Whittington at Fitzwarren's Stores.

**The Dame** — The Dame in this Panto is usually the Cook and is traditionally called Sarah the Cook, though on occasions she has been given other names; she works for Alderman Fitzwarren.

**Idle Jack** — He is the Simple Simon and Goodie of the piece and so the communicator with the audience, he is much loved by all the children.

**Good Fairy** — The most common and current name given to this Fairy is, Fairy Bowbells, and like all Good Fairies in Panto Land she is instrumental in making Dick's dreams come true, and in turning wrong to right and evil to good.

**Baddie** — In this Panto the Baddie – or Villain of the piece, as he is frequently known – traditionally goes by the name of King Rat. He turns up anywhere and everywhere, just to make things as difficult as possible for Dick and his Cat.

**Captain and Mate** — These two comedians turn up on the *Saucy Sally*, Alderman Fitzwarren's ship. Now the names for this pair of comedic characters each year changes from Panto to Panto which is great for the writer(s) and director of a Panto as it gives variety and often a current feel to the piece.

# THE PANTO STORYLINE OF *DICK WHITTINGTON*

*Once upon a time …* Dick Whittington, a poor boy, who having been told that the streets of London are paved with gold sets, off to seek his fortune. But when he arrives in London he finds that not only is he as penniless as he was when he set out, but that he is now friendless too, friendless that is until the Good Fairy Bowbells introduces him to Tommy the Cat.

Dick and his new friend, Tommy, then find work in Fitzwarren's Stores, owned by the merchant Alderman Fitzwarren; also working at Fitzwarren's is Sarah the Cook and Idle Jack. Whilst there Dick falls in love with Alice Fitzwarren, the Alderman's daughter, and all goes well until the Alderman trusts Dick with the important job of guarding his safe overnight.

King Rat, the Villain of the Panto, is like all villains in Panto Land and turns up whenever things are going right for the hero, and so now that Dick has a job, has a girl and is a trusted young man seems to be the ideal opportunity for the Villain to put in an appearance, and he doesn't disappoint us! He fools Dick and steals the money, entrusted in his keeping, from the safe, which he then duly puts into Dick's pocket thus ensuring

*Dick Whittington*, a Panto based on fact.

that he will get the blame when the crime is discovered. His plan works and when the money is found in Dick's pocket he loses his job, his friends and, worst of all, Alice, whom the Alderman says he must never see again. Dick and Tommy the Cat are then banished from London in disgrace. But the Good Fairy Bowbells is not far away and has other plans.

When Dick and Tommy reach Highgate Hill on their journey out of London, they turn to look at the City for one last time. It is then that Dick hears the bells of London calling out to him, to turn back. They seem to be saying: 'Turn again Whittington, Lord Mayor of London'. He is told that if he faces his troubles and heads back to London then he will become Lord Mayor – not just once, but three times. Dick Whittington and his Cat then turn around and head back to the City.

When he returns to London, though, he does not go to Fitzwarren's but heads straight for the docks. He and Tommy stow away on the ship *Saucy Sally*, which just so happens to be owned by Alderman Fitzwarren and which is due to set sail. When at sea, a storm brews up and the ship sinks – a good excuse for colourful underwater scenes! Eventually, all the ship's passengers and crew are washed ashore in Morocco, where no one has ever seen a cat before and so Tommy the Cat causes quite a stir.

They soon discover that the Sultan of Morocco's palace would appear to be over-run with rats – and all the fault of King Rat, of course, the Villain who turns up anywhere and everywhere and this leads the Sultan to promise that whoever rids him of the plague of rats will be rewarded with half of his Kingdom. Cue Dick to offer the services of Tommy, who of course disposes of all the rats and so, when the Sultan honours his promise, Dick becomes an extremely wealthy man and as a result is able to return to London where he meets with Alice once more and is reconciled with her father who gives his consent to their marriage. The Panto ends with the marriage of Dick and Alice – and, of course, with Dick as Lord Mayor of London and so ... *everyone lives happily ever after.*

## AND FINALLY

- On Highgate Hill in London, on the site where Dick Whittington supposedly heard the bells of London calling him back to become, 'Three times Lord Mayor', you can see a statue of his cat – though to be honest it is not certain that he ever had a cat – standing in front of Whittington

Hospital. Authentic? Who knows and frankly who cares! Romantic? Certainly is, and we love it

- I have to say here that I have always found it quite sad that the villain of the piece should be called 'King Rat', bearing in mind the fact this is the title of the chief Water Rat elected each year in that wonderful Grand Order of the Water Rats, an organisation made up almost exclusively of entertainers, which does good and charitable works

# *PUSS IN BOOTS* THE PANTOMIME

## ORIGINS

The origins of the tale of Puss in Boots was related in *Histories ou Contes du Temps Passé* by Perrault, which was first published in 1697, and is the oft (a bit dated!) used rags to riches style of tale. However, it is not quite that straightforward for Perrault based his story on an older Italian folk tale, and

*Puss in Boots* the Pantomime – just look at those costumes; how things have changed!

63

he did not create the cat – what is it with these cats! No one is sure whether Dick Whittington ever had a cat and in the original tale of Puss in Boots there was no cat either. This would seem to substantiate my mother's theory of 'Never trust a cat!' She used to say that they are independent creatures and a law unto themselves, telling me that a cat will be where it wants to be and not where you think it should be. And she was clearly quite right – just like mothers always are! With cats just turning up in our Pantos, as and when they feel like it!

## FIRST PRODUCTION

The first recorded production of *Puss in Boots* was in 1817, in Covent Garden, and featured the great Joseph Grimaldi. However, it was not a success – perhaps a warning of things to come, for this has never been one of the most popular Pantos and in fact is produced less and less as the years pass by.

## CHARACTERS INCLUDE

In this particular Panto there would appear to be no set of traditional names as in other Pantos, and so one wonders whether this could perhaps in the past have contributed to the limited success of the storyline, and so in turn the Panto itself? After all, as we have previously seen, predictability is a huge and important part of the Panto experience? And surely the predictability element must include not only the characters, but their names too – just a thought.

| | |
|---|---|
| Principal Boy | Generally, the Principal Boy is called Colin, though there have been variations over the years. |
| Principal Girl | There are many variations here on the subject of her name – certainly too many to mention. |
| The Cat | The Puss in Boots character, who appears first as a cat – actor in skins – until he is transformed into a walking, talking human version of a Puss in Boots, has no specific name but one that varies according to the whim of the writer. |

| | |
|---|---|
| The Dame | Unlike in most other Panto productions, the Dame in *Puss in Boots* does not have a traditional name and so yet again 'her' name varies according to what the writer wants. |
| The Comic | Once more a variety of names has been given to the comic character, but of course in this case he is still loved by the children, whatever his name! |
| The Baddie | In this Production the Baddie is an Ogre – of various names, of course. |
| The Good Fairy | At least some things have remained traditional and although the plot is not based on magic, there is at least generally a Good Fairy – though not always. |
| Baddies' Sidekicks | Again of various names. |

It is so sad that the lack of predictability even makes for a disappointing read, does it not!

## THE PANTO STORYLINE OF *PUSS IN BOOTS*

*Once upon a time* … the local Miller died, and Colin found that in his will he had been left a cat, which did little to impress him, especially as his brothers had inherited so much more. Never-the-less, he set off to find his fortune, with his Cat in tow, of course.

Colin's fortune changes when he buys his Cat some boots – now don't ask why Colin would want his Cat to wear boots, for this is Panto Land where nothing makes sense, where anything can, and where it usually does, happen. It is after he puts on the boots that the Cat turns into a magical Cat, and this new Cat then sets about trying to persuade various people that his master is actually something he is not – and that is someone from a higher class of society. On the pretence that he is a man of wealth Colin wins the love of the King's daughter, the King of course being totally unaware that his daughter is in love with a penniless wanderer.

## AND FINALLY

- Professional productions of *Puss in Boots* are rarely seen today, but despite this I do believe that it still deserves to be in the list of traditional and true Pantos as it is only in frequent years that it has slipped so much from favour
- The actual story line – as the character's names – also changes so frequently that it is impossible to give here an extended and solid storyline as we did with the other Pantos

# *JACK AND THE BEANSTALK* THE PANTOMIME

## ORIGINS

There lived in Cornwall a Giant – according to the legend of *Jack the Giant Killer* – who frightened the locals with his antics of stealing and taking away their cattle. Living in this area, near Land's End, there happened to be the son of a farmer, who went by the name of Jack. It was Jack who trapped and killed the Giant. It is in this legend that the Panto *Jack and the Beanstalk* has its very early roots, although the beanstalk was not a part of the original legend and neither were the magic beans, both of which were added at a later date. It is in fact a story that took many centuries to evolve and develop into the Panto we know and love today.

Jack and the Beanstalk.

## FIRST PRODUCTION

*Jack and the Beanstalk* was first produced as a Panto at Drury Lane in 1819 when an actress by the name of Eliza Povey played the part of Jack – and so you see the tradition of a female taking the part of the male principal lead really does go back centuries.

## CHARACTERS INCLUDE

Jack

The title role, Jack's surname is generally Trott, though sometimes he is known as Jack Durden.

Dame

The Dame in this Panto plays the part of Jack's mother and so is called either Dame Trott or Dame Durden.

Comic

The Comic role is generally Jack's brother, who goes by the name of Simon (the Simple Simon of the piece).

Cow

This is the 'skins' part; the cow generally goes by the name Buttercup or more often by the name of Daisy, although some writers prefer to 'invent' their own names.

Principal Girl

She is often the daughter of the Squire, sometimes the King, though to be honest it does seem a little far-fetched for the King to be living in a village with the commoners! Sometimes the Principal Girl is fittingly called Jill, which thrills the younger children (Jack and Jill!).

Squire/King

The Squire does not have a traditional name and so the writers have a free rein leaving his name open to interpretation, the same applies if the writers decide he is a King.

Good Fairy

The name given to the Good Fairy in this Panto generally has something to do with the garden, and so you may easily come across names such as Tulip.

Giant

The traditional name for the giant in Jack and the Beanstalk is Blunderbore, though some writers prefer a variation on this.

| Giant's Henchman | The traditional name given to this character is Fleshcreep, though of course this is open to change and variation, and we mustn't forget of course that there could well be two of them as a double act, thus becoming the Giant's Henchmen. However, this is more likely to happen on the amateur circuit where the only added expense of having two henchmen would be an extra costume, and the extra bums on seats he would bring in as his supporters would soon pay for that! |

## THE PANTO STORYLINE OF *JACK AND THE BEANSTALK*

*Once upon a time* ... a Giant by the name of Blunderbore was terrorising a village with his constant demands for food, cattle and money – not to mention the kidnapping of some of the villagers. Living in the village is the hero of the piece, Jack, who is in love with the King/Squire's daughter and when the King announces the hand of his daughter in marriage to whoever slays the Giant, Jack seizes his chance – one does wonder whether the Princess had any say in the matter.

Jack lives in the village with his widowed mother, Dame Trott, his brother Simple Simon and the lovable Buttercup/Daisy or whatever, the Cow, and like all other villagers they have no money left at all. Desperate, Dame Trott announces that she will have to sell the cow – whom I am from now on going to call Buttercup for the purpose of this piece. On the way to the market where Jack is going to sell Buttercup, he meets Fleshcreep, the Baddie of the piece who offers to buy the cow for a bag of Magic Beans. Jack agrees and hands over his more than reluctant bovine friend.

It is not only Buttercup, however, who has been taken by Fleshcreep for it would seem that so too has the Princess. Even more reason for Jack to find, fight and kill the Giant, but not before he faces the wrath of his mother, who is not at all happy to hear that her son has sold her best friend, Buttercup, to one of the Giant's men ... for a bag of beans! Furious, she throws the beans out of the window. Of course, when everyone wakes up on the very next morning the 'magic' beans have grown into a gigantic beanstalk. And, of course, what else can Jack do but climb the Beanstalk, which he does.

When he reaches the top, not only does he find himself outside the Giant's castle, but when he looks behind him he realises that both his mother and brother, Simple Simon, have followed him up the beanstalk; in some versions of the Panto, even the King has followed him too! Now enter the Giant with the well-known cry of: 'Fee-fi-fo-fum, I smell the blood of an English man!' Jack then discovers that the Giant's castle is full of treasures, such as a singing harp and a hen that lays golden eggs. But whilst he is interested in these, he is more interested in finding the Princess and Buttercup the cow, which of course he does. He also defeats Fleshcreep in a brawl, slays the Giant, descends the Beanstalk with the Giant's treasure, his mother, brother, Princess and Buttercup – oh, and the King if he actually went up there in the first place. He then rushes off to find an axe with which he cuts down the enormous Beanstalk, just in case any stray giants decide to pay him a visit. Wealth is restored to the village, Jack marries his Princess and so once again ... *everyone lived happily ever after.*

## AND FINALLY

• Have you ever wondered why you don't get to see this Panto quite so often as the others? Well, it is quite simply the most difficult to create because the set – and the people – all have to be to scale. After all children have to see a real Giant and not some cobbled together job!

## *SLEEPING BEAUTY* THE PANTOMIME

## ORIGINS

The story upon which the Panto *Sleeping Beauty* can be found in Charles Perrault's fairy tale *La Belle au Bois Dormant*. Generally, the Panto version is pretty true to Perrault's original tale, which was first published in the late seventeenth century and at one time was one of the most popular of the traditional Pantos. Although in recent years its popularity has waned somewhat, there does seem to be a rekindled interest of late as more and more companies choose this as their annual seasonal offering.

## FIRST PRODUCTION

The first Panto version of the Sleeping Beauty story was at Drury Lane in 1806 and was called *The Sleeping Beauty: A Grand Legendary Melodrama*.

## CHARACTERS INCLUDE

| | |
|---|---|
| Princess | Perrault called his Princess Aurora, and so many production companies choose to stick with this, although over time there have been variations on this, the most popular of which is Princess Beauty – well, I suppose it does make sense! However, there is no hard and fast rule dictating her name and so variations abound. |
| Prince | As with the Princess, there is no traditional name for the Prince, although again most companies stick to, or a close variation on, Perrault's name for him which is Florimond. |
| Dame | The role of the Dame generally falls upon the Queen or upon the nanny/nursemaid of the Princess and again has no traditional name, thus giving the producer and or writer artistic licence to call her whatever takes their fancy, something they always love. |
| King | Another writer's dream character, for again he has no traditional name. |
| Good Fairy | Generally, she is referred to quite simply as the Good Fairy, though sometimes she is called the Fairy Godmother and on other occasions, again, any name that takes the writer/director/producer's fancy. |
| Bad Fairy | She goes under a variety of names too – and frequently under no name at all, just being called 'The Witch' which, strictly speaking, is actually incorrect for she is in fact the eighth and forgotten Fairy, turned evil. |
| The Comic | The chief comic in Sleeping Beauty is often the court jester; sometimes he is a page at the court and sometimes he works in the kitchens. A popular name for this character is Muddles. |

## THE PANTO STORYLINE OF *SLEEPING BEAUTY*

*Once upon a time …* a beautiful and much–longed for daughter was born to a childless King and Queen who then arranged a lavish christening to which they invited all the known fairies in their Kingdom. Sadly though, they knew of only seven fairies, when there were in fact eight in their Kingdom; this eighth fairy, Uglyane, had shut herself away for fifty years, and for that reason her very existence had been forgotten by all. However, by not inviting this eighth and 'forgotten' fairy they had in fact sealed the fate of their beloved baby daughter.

A place was set at the christening banquet for each of the seven invited fairies, who in turn brought a gift for the new baby Princess. There then arrived at the christening banquet one unexpected and uninvited guest, an old crone, for whom no place was set. This old crone in fact was the eighth fairy. Despite her anger at been forgotten, she was treated kindly by the King and Queen and a place was immediately set for her. The eighth fairy, however, was not so courteous and instead of bestowing a gift upon the baby Princess she granted to her only a wicked curse before leaving the banquet to return once more to her isolated existence. This curse being that when the Princess reached her 16th birthday she would prick her finger on a spindle (the sharp point of a spinning wheel), and die.

However, thankfully, seated next to the eighth fairy was the Fairy Hippolyta and, hearing the bitter old crone muttering, she feared that she would do harm to the baby Princess when her turn came to bestow a gift. As a result, Hippolyta had earlier left the table and hidden herself behind

Sleeping Beauty – just look at the hair! Would little girls aspire to this look now? I think not!

71

the curtain awaiting Uglyane's gift. So, when this evil gift is bestowed upon the sleeping baby, Hippolyta tells the stricken court that, although she cannot reverse the spell of Uglyane, she can in fact alter it. And so it was that Hippolyta ensured that the sleeping baby, with her blessing, would not die, but would merely sleep for a long period of time – apparently a hundred years – only to be woken by the kiss of a handsome Prince who she said would also fall in love with her.

From thereon, the King bans all spinning wheels from the castle, but one old servant is unaware of this ban and so when the 16-year-old Princess Aurora stumbles across the old woman spinning, she is fascinated and so is invited to try her hand at it. Of course, she pricks her finger and falls to the ground, apparently dead. The alarm is sounded and Fairy Hippolyta arrives at the castle to cast a spell over the court as well. As a result it is deemed that all within the palace walls will also sleep until the Princess is woken by a kiss from a handsome Prince.

A hundred years pass and the castle is hidden by undergrowth and almost forgotten by all – all that is except Prince Florimond and his father, who hear of the legend. The Prince declares that he will be the one to rescue the Princess from her enforced sleep. Prince Florimond reaches the tower, discovers the sleeping Princess and awakens her – and the entire palace – with a kiss. Of course, they fall in love, marry and upon the abdication of their fathers from their own respective Kingdoms the two Kingdoms become one, the Prince and Princess rule and … everyone lives happily ever after.

## AND FINALLY

- *Sleeping Beauty* was once the most popular of all the Pantos but has now actually been usurped by that other Panto favourite, *Cinderella*

## *MOTHER GOOSE* THE PANTOMIME

## ORIGINS

The origin of this Panto is not quite as straightforward as some of the other Pantos, with the earliest recorded mention of Mother Goose being in 1650 in France, when Jean Loret mentioned her in his book *La Muse Historique*.

Then in 1697 Charles Perrault used the phrase in his published collection of eight fairy tales *Histories and Tales of Long Ago, with Morals*. His book showed an old lady spinning and telling stories and in 1729 it was published in England under the title *Mother Goose's Fairy Tales* and ever since the name Mother Goose has been widely used for various collections of folk tales and especially for collections of nursery rhymes, and so it became an umbrella term too and not simply the title of a single tale.

Pity the poor actor/actress in the skins?

## FIRST PRODUCTION

One of the first recorded productions of *Mother Goose – Harlequin and Mother Goose; or the Golden Egg –* was as early as 1806 and featured the great Joseph Grimaldi. This production, however, bore little resemblance to the Panto we know today for the birth of today's *Mother Goose* was not until the beginning of the twentieth century when J. Hickory Wood created the Panto for that other great performer Dan Leno.

## CHARACTERS INCLUDE

| | |
|---|---|
| The Goose | The Goose is this Panto is traditionally called Priscilla and is, of course, the 'skin' part in the Panto. |
| The Dame | The Dame traditionally takes the name of Mother Goose, although some writers do like to give her a Christian name too. |
| Principal Boy | He is often Mother Goose's son – though in some productions he is someone else's son, anyone's it would seem! Tradition says that his name should be Colin, but sadly he has been given other names. And |

just for the record – I hate it when traditions are ignored, as I am sure you have worked out by now!

Principal Girl | Here the traditional name for the Principal Girl is Jill and she is often the Squire's daughter, but when Colin is not Mother Goose's son then sometimes Jill is her daughter.

Comic | The comedian of the piece is usually the Dame's son and is called Billy – Billy Goose – he is sometimes known as Silly Billy, which of course the children in the audience love.

The Squire | This is the character usually responsible for demanding money from Mother Goose; he is called Squire and then whatever second name the writer wants to call him – Squire Gimmee, for example, 'Gimmee your money, or else'.

The Good Fairy | She is what she is, a Good Fairy, and the name varies according to whatever the writer fancies.

The Villain | Usually called the Demon King, though this role has on occasions has been played by a woman, in which case the villain becomes the Demon Queen.

The Goose King | Also sometimes known as King Gander, his role in the plot is to preside over the trial.

The Brokers Men | Also known as the Bailiffs, they are frequently the rent collectors for the Squire.

The Maid | Sometimes there will be a maid character as a sidekick for Mother Goose.

## THE PANTO STORYLINE OF *MOTHER GOOSE*

*Once upon a time* … the Demon King challenges the Good Fairy saying: 'Search all the world, and you will fail to find a man or woman with contented mind'. He then gives the Dame of the Panto a magical goose who she christens Ann Priscilla Mary May and who becomes a much-loved part of her family. She is then given wealth and having that she craves beauty, there's no pleasing some people is there!

As a result of her crabbing, the Demon tempts her to enter the 'Pool of Beauty', but in return she must give up the one thing she holds dear to her – Priscilla the Goose. So to gain beauty, she sacrifices everything.

It then takes the rest of the Panto for the Dame to understand that looks count for very little in the great scheme of things and that it is not what you *are* but what you *feel* that matters, that and the love of a true and loyal friend. She comes to realise that she has lost everything and gained nothing as she fights to win back her Goose. In the end Good triumphs over Evil in this very simple Panto and ... *everyone lived happily ever after.*

## AND FINALLY

• The part of the Goose is probably the most difficult of skin roles in Panto, and is without doubt the most uncomfortable!

*Chapter 3*

# AND THE OTHER PANTOMIMES – WHAT ARE THEY?

We have now looked at the most popular and traditional of the Pantos; some would say the *only* Pantos. But the truth of the matter is that they are in fact *not* the only Pantos available for production, for there are others and so it is now time to have a brief look at these other less popular Pantos, again some would say those actually masquerading as Pantos!

Into this category fall Pantos such as:

• *Babes in the Wood/ Robin Hood*
• *Goldilocks and the Three Bears*
• *Goody Two Shoes*
• *Hop O' My Thumb*
• *Peter Pan*
• *Robinson Crusoe*
• *Little Red Riding Hood*

Of these, the ones you are most likely to catch as a production are: *Babes in the Wood/ Robin Hood*, *Goldilocks and the Three Bears* and *Peter Pan*, with productions of the others being more difficult. Having said that though, amateur dramatic societies are quite often a good hunting ground when out in search of the more obscure Panto storylines, for they are hugely competitive and less interested in financial profit. In most cases their one aim is to keep their society solvent, whilst at the same time outdoing the nearest rival society in terms of originality.

# BABES IN THE WOOD/ROBIN HOOD

## ORIGINS

The Panto story of *Babes in the Wood* is based on an old English ballad of 1595, called *The Children in The Wood: or, the Norfolk Gentleman's Last Will and Testament*. This ballad, which is now preserved in the British Museum, tells the story of a wealthy widower who left his children in the care of his brother. The children's wicked uncle then employed 'two ruffians' to take his charges into a wood where he instructed him to kill them.

> He bargained with two ruffians strong,
> Who were of furious mood,
> That they should take these children young
> And slaye them in a wood.

One of these 'ruffians', however, took pity on the children and, instead of killing them, he murdered his companion. Leaving the children alone in the wood, he then went off on the pretence of searching for food. Of course, he never returned and although the children survived for a while by eating wild berries, they eventually died in each other's arms and a Robin Redbreast covered their bodies with leaves.

> In one another's arms they died
> Awanting due relief:
> No burial this pretty pair
> Of any man receives,
> Till Robin redbreast piously
> Did cover them with leaves.

It is easy to see that the story of the Babes is actually quite thin to stand on a stage and captivate children for 2½ hours and so in 1867 Robin Hood was introduced into the storyline; this filled in two gaps. It meant that the Panto could be extended in length and that Robin could rescue the two children so that in true Panto fashion ... *everyone could then live happily ever after.*

## THE PANTO STORYLINE OF *BABES IN THE WOOD*

After the Babes are deserted in the forest by their Wicked Uncle's Henchmen they are discovered by Robin Hood and Maid Marian who take them to their encampment, where in some versions Maid Marian then becomes their Nurse. In this version Robin is Principal Boy and Maid Marian is the Principal Girl; the Sheriff of Nottingham usually plays the Wicked Uncle and of course there are plenty of Merry Men to play all the other parts and provide the fun and frolic expected in a Panto; more unconventional than traditional, this is a Panto that is not staged as often as some of the others.

## AND FINALLY

- Historically, Robin Hood actually lived 200 years before the Babes were born but this is the world of Panto where anything goes and everything is believable – when you want to believe!

## GOLDILOCKS AND THE THREE BEARS

### ORIGINS

It would seem at first glance that the origin of this Panto is quite straightforward in that it is taken from the classic fairy tale of *Goldilocks and the Three Bears*, but what indeed is the origin of the fairy tale? It is not quite so simple, for it would appear to be an amalgamation of various sources from an old Scottish folktale to a children's story taken from Robert Southey's book *Doctor*, which was published in 1837, through to the Brothers Grimm version in their collection of folk tales. Even the character of Goldilocks herself has changed over the years and she has morphed from an old woman into a young girl with golden hair.

### THE PANTO STORYLINE OF *GOLDILOCKS AND THE THREE BEARS*

For the purposes of a Panto the story itself is in fact too short and too simple and so has been added to in a variety of ways, although most do seem to revolve around a circus theme – whilst of course keeping the simplicity intact, that of a young girl with golden locks who stumbles across a cottage belonging to three bears – Daddy Bear, Mummy Bear and Baby Bear, with all their proportionally sized belongings, which never fails to delight the imagination of children in the audience. The reason for incorporating a circus into the storyline is quite obviously the animal content – however else could three bears be included into a plot other than in a circus!

## AND FINALLY

• Although not one of the major and most popular of Pantos, *Goldilocks and the Three Bears* has survived into the twenty-first century when it is still being produced. It was a popular Panto in Victorian times with a very early version presented in 1852 at Her Majesty's Theatre in London. W.S. Gilbert (of Gilbert and Sullivan) wrote a version in 1867 which played at the Lyceum Theatre, also in London

## *GOODY TWO SHOES*

Although one of the most popular of the Victorian Pantos, *Goody Two Shoes* has now been confined to the archives and is rarely brought out and into production. So, if you are lucky enough to see a production take note, for the chances are that you may never see it again!

## ORIGINS

The history of the Goody Two Shoes story is that it was a nursery tale which was first published in 1765. Who wrote it is unproven, though many think it was written by Oliver Goldsmith who apparently had come across a young girl from one of London's Ragged Schools. This young girl was in a hurry, excited by the fact that she had been given a pair of shoes as a reward for being a good girl. The intervention of the fairies, it would seem, was a later addition.

## THE PANTO STORYLINE OF *GOODY TWO SHOES*

The central characters of the piece are two orphans, Margery and her brother Tommy. They are poor in the extreme in the fact that poor little

Margery has only one shoe to her name instead of the necessary two! It is the very simple story of good winning through when a fairy cobbler takes pity on the poor, young orphan and makes her a pair of magic shoes, though it is in fact often made more complicated by producers wanting to spice it up a bit. After Margery acquires two shoes she goes on to do many good deeds, marries well and, of course, *everyone lives happily ever after.*

## AND FINALLY

- One of the earliest versions of *Goody Two Shoes* was staged at Sadler's Wells in 1803

# HOP O' MY THUMB

I have in the past heard this particular Panto being referred to as the 'mongrel' of Pantos, due to the inclusion of elements of various other Pantos such as *Jack and the Beanstalk* and *Babes in the Wood*.

## ORIGINS

*Hop O' My Thumb* was one of the last stories in the collection of the Mother Goose fairy tales, which were written by Charles Perrault and published in 1697. Originally, it wasn't actually called *Hop O' My Thumb*, but was entitled *Le Petit Poucet* and remained so until 1764 when it became known in the UK as *Little Thumb*; it wasn't until 1804 that the title *Hop O' My Thumb* was first used.

## THE PANTO STORYLINE OF *HOP O' MY THUMB*

There have been so few productions of this Panto that to find the definitive version of the storyline is virtually impossible. However, what we do know is that productions are based around the central character of Hop O' My Thumb, a name inspired by his diminutive size. He was small enough in fact to hop onto a man's thumb! Hop is the youngest of the seven stepsons of Surley Thumb, a poor woodcutter who cooks up a plan to rid himself of the children he considers a hindrance by losing them in the wood – with echoes of Hansel and Gretel. Lost in the wood, the children stumble upon a castle inhabited by the Giant Fee FoFum – with echoes of Jack and the

Beanstalk. There then generally ensues a plot that would confuse the brightest of buttons – and I don't mean Cinderella's friend either – but which in general ends *happily ever after.*

## AND FINALLY

- This is a Panto that is now virtually extinct – if Pantos can be extinct, that is!
- In 1913 *Hop O' My Thumb* was taken by the Drury Lane Company to America where it was produced at the Manhattan Theatre in New York

## *PETER PAN*

This is a production that always falls right in the middle of the controversy: 'Is it a Panto or is it a Christmas story?' As there seems no end in sight to this argument, I think for my own personal safety I shall keep my counsel on this one!

## ORIGINS

I don't think there is a man, woman or child who has not heard of the magical character Peter Pan, who was created by the author J.M. Barrie. The story of this character is now presented annually as a Christmas entertainment at many venues throughout the UK, but whether it qualifies as a Panto must be left, I fear, as an on-going argument.

The play *Peter Pan* had its first showing at the Duke of York's Theatre, London on 27 December 1904 and has continued to run in one form or another ever since. Of course, children are enthralled by the fact that not only did Peter Pan refuse to grow up, but that he could fly too, and what child has never fantasised about flying! Actresses too clamour for the tomboy role, though of course one has to be of a rather petite stature to qualify.

When presented as 'a Christmas Entertainment/Panto' the story it would seem always stays true to the original storyline and so to include some of the stock Panto characters is virtually impossible. Some Peter Pan Pantos have though tried to introduce a Dame character to the plot through the Nursemaid, though it is debatable whether it works or not.

## THE PANTO STORYLINE OF *PETER PAN*

Peter Pan doesn't want to grow up and so he runs away from home. One night he visits the home of the Darling family who live in Bloomsbury. Peter Pan has a fairy attendant called Tinker Bell and both of them can fly – not unusual for a fairy, but it is for a boy! Adventures then follow when he teaches the three Darling children to fly too, enabling them to go with him to Neverland, where he lives with the Lost Boys who are protected by a tribe of Red Indians.

Wendy, one of the Darling children, becomes mother to the Lost Boys, but one day when Peter is away they are all captured by the Pirate Captain Hook. Peter comes to the rescue and Hook is eaten by a crocodile. Peter then takes Wendy and her brothers home and, after declining an offer of adoption by Mrs Darling, he leaves with the promise that Wendy will visit him every year to do the spring-cleaning. Of course, in the Panto version *everyone lives happily ever after, including the Lost Boys.*

## AND FINALLY

*Peter Pan* premiered in America at the Empire Theatre, New York on 6 November 1905

# *ROBINSON CRUSOE*

This is another of the less popular, or should I say non-traditional Pantos, although it does often find favour with some of the amateur dramatic societies. Possibly this is because it is better for them not to be in competition with the large, commercial and professional producers; it is certainly better for the audiences, for they get to see a greater variety of Pantos on offer.

## ORIGINS

The Panto *Robinson Crusoe* is based on the novel of the same name which was written by Daniel Defoe and published in 1719. Defoe in turn gathered his inspiration from the true story of a sailor by the name of Alexander Selkirk, who found himself stranded on the desert island of Mas-a-Tierra, off Chile; the island was later renamed Robinson Crusoe Island. It is thought, too, that he gained further inspiration from the tales of another castaway, going by the name of Henry Pitman.

## THE PANTO STORYLINE OF *ROBINSON CRUSOE*

The basic Panto storyline is taken from Defoe's novel of the same name, though with many additions and variations, all of which are necessary to alleviate the boredom of watching one man shipwrecked alone on a desert island for an entire production, not to mention the necessity of introducing 'stock' characters in order for it actually to 'qualify' as a Panto! But still, given all of this, *Robinson Crusoe* is the story of one man shipwrecked on a desert island.

One man, that is, plus Mrs Crusoe, Polly Perkins, Will Atkins and Silly Billy, to name but a few – not to mention the odd goat, parrot and ape as the animal interests! Of course, in the Panto Robinson Crusoe is shipwrecked, but not so much alone and left to survive, but alone only until the others arrive. It is only a short while then before the rest of the 'cast' put in an appearance. Well, all things are possible in Panto Land after all. Robinson Crusoe also stumbles across footprints in the sand which lead him to the obligatory Man Friday, whilst the surrounding sea allows for great underwater, UV, scenes. The plots then vary to include buried treasure, pirates, cannibals and naturally a wedding to close. Quite what Daniel Defoe would have made of all this, I dread to think! In fact, and to be honest, one can really only say, 'The Panto *Robinson Crusoe* is *loosely* based on the novel of the same name by Daniel Defoe'.

## AND FINALLY

• It is said that Daniel Defoe named the hero of his novel Robinson Crusoe after he saw the name on a gravestone. Daniel Defoe was actually born Daniel Foe

## LITTLE RED RIDING HOOD

### ORIGINS

This tale, it would appear, has a variety of origins and some versions date as far back as Roman times, whilst other versions surface in eleventh-century France and, of course, as one would expect Charles Perrault and the Brothers Grimm had their own versions too. The earliest Panto version of Little Red Riding Hood is recorded as being at the beginning of the nineteenth century.

### THE PANTO STORYLINE OF *LITTLE RED RIDING HOOD*

Little Red Riding Hood's name derives from the fact that she always wears a bright-red cape and is doing so as usual on the day that she visits her Grandmother, who lives deep in the forest. Unknown to her, she is spotted by a wolf who goes ahead of her to reach Little Red Riding Hood's Grandmother's house before she does. Hey, this is Panto land and not only can wolves talk, but they are mind-readers too; how else would this particular wolf know to where Little Red Riding Hood was actually heading? Once there he either eats or locks up the Grandmother – depending on the wishes of the director in question – and then he dresses in her clothes, settles himself in her bed and awaits for the arrival of the unsuspecting little girl. Once Little Red Riding Hood arrives at the cottage there follows some of the most famous lines in the history of fairy tales when during somewhat of an altercation the confused little girl questions the size of various parts of her grandmother's anatomy.

| | |
|---|---|
| Little RRH: | Grandmother, what big ears you have! |
| Wolf: | All the better to hear you with! |
| Little RRH: | Grandmother, what big eyes you have! |
| Wolf: | All the better to see you with! |
| Little RRH: | Grandmother, what big teeth you have |
| Wolf: | All the better to eat you with! |

This does, of course, beg the question why Red Riding Hood didn't smell a rat, or at the very least a wolf! But to the delight of children everywhere she didn't and so the Wolf was free to pounce in an attempt to eat the little girl. The children love this potentially gruesome event, but are generally spared the trauma by the arrival of a woodsman (the Principal Boy) who saves Little Red Riding, rescues the Grandmother and converts the Wolf into a good guy!

## AND FINALLY

- It was this Panto that was chosen as the last Panto to be staged at Covent Garden

Look carefully at this photo and you will see that it takes more than just performers to put on a good Panto production.

*Chapter 4*

# GREAT BRITISH DAMES PAST AND PRESENT

Every profession has its experts, and every arm of every profession has its experts too. Panto is a branch of that great business we call 'Show' and so quite rightly has its own field of experts who know, or knew, more than the rest of us about this arm of the theatrical family. Some say that a Panto Dame is just a feller in a frock, but they couldn't be more wrong for a Panto Dame is no less than a British institution.

The theatrical tradition of men playing women can be traced way back to a time when it was thought inappropriate for 'ladies' to act, and so it was that the men played all the female roles as well as their own. Even in Shakespeare's plays all of the female roles were played by young boys and this is why quite often as a part of the plot the young female lead must dress up as a man, thus giving the young boy playing the part the opportunity to play within his own gender for a large section of the performance. Even when actresses were established on the stage it would often be the case that an older actor would be brought in to play the older or comedic female roles as the young women were interested only in the younger and more glamorous parts.

To some, Panto is just flippant fun and not to be taken seriously. On a personal level I find such an attitude an insult, for entertainment is just that – entertainment – and if some decide that a good night out is to be had shouting 'He's behind you' at their local theatre, then that is fine by me. And if someone else wants to be educated in the social disadvantage of being a black, gay and disabled individual in a selfish society, then that is equally fine by me too. What right has any one person to judge the integrity of another, especially based on what type of entertainment they prefer? I will now get off my soapbox – and yes it is something I feel quite strongly about – and carry on talking about the art of Panto.

I find it fascinating to listen to an expert, as opposed to an enthusiast, talk about their love of this, that or the other, for it is the experts who rattle on at a hundred miles an hour spouting an unending font of knowledge about their 'baby' to anyone and everyone, where people may hear, but no one listens – except me perhaps. I don't necessarily understand, of course, but never-the-less I am always in awe of experts; oh alright, and a little envious too!

Panto has, like all other subjects, a rich bank of such experts, both past and present, and quite often these experts are the Panto Dames. I would like to say why this is the case; why the Dames have become the experts and not one of the other characters. But to be honest I don't really know why it is so, I just know that the Dames in general love their art to such an extent that they have, almost without exception, become masters in their field. And it is just a small selection of these experts who will feature in this section of the book. You may not agree with those I have chosen and may in fact have preferred to see other names adorn these pages, but I am never-the-less confident that even if you as the reader would have made alternative choices, you will still no doubt agree with me that those chosen certainly know their stuff! So who are they and just why have I chosen them? Well, in no particular order we have Joseph Grimaldi, the famous clown whose name Joseph (Joey) gave rise to the name by which clowns are still known to this day. He is also credited with the creation of the traditional clown make-up, but more importantly with the creation of the Panto Dame which is now such an integral part of the whole to the extent that Panto wouldn't now be Panto without an appearance from the Dame. Then, much later on, we have Roy Hudd; he has become a national institution and is famous as a stand-up comedian, a writer, an actor and of course a real authority on Panto. Although he doesn't actually play the part of Dame year in and year out, he has to be in this book because what he doesn't know about Panto just isn't worth knowing. To be honest, I struggled with where to 'put him', but I concluded I would put him with the greatest and the best, for that is where he belongs! Also included in this section is Christopher Biggins, known quite simply as 'Biggins', who epitomises the very word Panto. I could go on and on, but far better that you read on instead!

As far as the names given to the Dames, it is rather nice when they are traditional and you can go along to the Panto secure in the knowledge of what the Dame will actually be called. However, as we have just seen in the previous chapter, this is not always the case and so please enjoy the following, where we have just a few of the great British Dames both past and present.

# ARTHUR ASKEY CBE

*1900–82*
*Known as 'Big-hearted Arthur'*

## THE MAN AND HIS LIFE

- Arthur Askey was born on 6 June 1900 as Arthur Bowden Askey in Liverpool and was the eldest child of Samuel Askey and Betsy Bowden
- He was educated in Liverpool and when he grew up only reached the height of 5ft 2in
- At the age of 16 years he started work as a clerk
- He served in the armed forces during the First World War
- When he was 24 years old he joined a concert party and started touring the halls
- In 1925 Askey married Elizabeth May Swash with whom he had a daughter, Anthea, born in 1933
- In the late 1930s the BBC radio show *Band Waggon* catapulted Arthur to fame and in the 1940s he appeared in many films
- In 1969 he was awarded the OBE
- In the 1970s he appeared as a panellist on the TV talent show *New Faces* – where he was always the kind member of the panel!
- In 1974 his wife, Elizabeth, died
- In 1981 he was awarded the CBE
- Arthur Askey died at the age of 82 on 16 November 1982

## AND FINALLY

- Just like our Brucie, Arthur Askey was well known for his catchphrases, the most famous of which included: 'Hello Playmates', 'Before your very eyes' and ' I thank you'
- He was known for his horn-rimmed glasses
- Circulatory problems resulted in the amputation of both his legs when gangrene set in

- His act was a silly act, full of silly jokes, silly dances and silly songs; his most well-known silly song was 'The Busy Bee Song' (the words to this song can be found in Chapter 7), which he performed whilst doing an equally silly dance! This song was generally sung whenever and wherever he appeared including in Panto. It was, what we would call today, his party piece, but I actually prefer the term 'signature tune' – more professional, and that is after all what he was – a professional

# BERWICK KALER

*Currently the UK's longest serving Dame, he has played at York Theatre Royal since 1977*

## THE MAN AND HIS LIFE

- Berwick Kaler was born as Raymond Kaler in 1946 in Sunderland as the youngest of seven children
- His father, who died when Berwick was just 2 years old, had the Christian name of Berwick and so Raymond took on this name, in honour of his father, when he entered the entertainment profession
- Until he was 2 years old the family lived in a one-bedroomed house with an outside toilet, which was quite 'normal' and acceptable at that time in the North East, working class area of the UK
- He was educated at St Mary's Roman Catholic School
- As a double blow his mother then died when he was just 11 years old
- At the age of 15 years he left the North East and went to London where he found a job as a painter and decorator
- A chance meeting with the movie actor Laurence Harvey made him want to try his hand at acting and so he simply bought the *Stage* newspaper, went out, got himself an audition and then a job; and the rest is history, as they say
- At the age of 19 he got a job in his first Panto, *Babes in the Wood*, at the Palace Theatre, Manchester
- He then went on to play a further six commercial Pantos in the part of the Villain, before taking on the role of Dame at York Theatre Royal. He could never have known at the time how this move was to shape his future life

- In 2002 he was awarded an honorary degree from York University
- York has also made him a Freeman of the City
- It would be easy to think of him as *just* a Panto Dame but over the years he has built up a very impressive and diverse stage and screen CV

## AND FINALLY

- Berwick Kaler has now completed over thirty-five seasons not only as a writer/director for the Panto at York theatre Royal, but also as the Dame
- The York Pantos are so good and renowned that they account for 40 per cent of the yearly ticket sales for the York Theatre Royal
- Pierce Brosnan was at one time on the stage-management team for a Berwick Kaler Panto at York, whilst Gary Oldman once played the Cat in *Dick Whittington*, and Mark Addy featured in *Sinbad the Sailor*

# CHRISTOPHER BIGGINS

*1948–*
*Hailed as a national treasure, he is affectionately and simply known as just 'Biggins', the performer who never stops smiling*

## THE MAN AND HIS LIFE

- Christopher Biggins was born on 16 December 1948 in Oldham, Lancashire
- He was raised and educated in Salisbury where his father had his own second-hand car sales business and his mother was a barmaid
- In Salisbury he was educated privately – and had elocution lessons too
- He started his professional training with Salisbury Rep after which he went on to Bristol Old Vic

Biggins in Panto regalia.

- In 1971 he married Beatrice Norbury; they later divorced in 1974
- In the 1970s he played the part of the Emperor Nero in the award-winning BBC1 TV series I *Claudius*
- It was in 1976 when he was just 28 years old that he was first offered a Panto
- In 1990 he played Herod in the musical *Jesus Christ Superstar* at the Barbican in London
- Now openly gay, in 2006 he formed a civil partnership with his partner, Neil Sinclair
- In 2007 he was crowned King of the Jungle when he won the seventh series of *I'm a Celebrity Get Me Out of Here*
- The year 2007 saw him touring with the *Rocky Horror Show* in which he played the Narrator

## AND FINALLY

- Christopher Biggins has always said that he has no regrets about declaring himself bankrupt in 1995; in fact to the contrary, he thinks it was the best thing he ever did
- His autobiography is called *Just Biggins*
- He is most well known in Panto Land for his portrayals of Widow Twankey in *Aladdin*
- Standing at 6ft 1in, Christopher Biggins makes for a tall and impressive Dame, and of course tradition does dictate that that this role must be played 'as obviously a man pretending to be a woman'

# DAN LENO

*1860–1904*
*Victorian music-hall performer who, along with Joseph Grimaldi, is considered to be one of the greatest Panto performers of all time*

## THE MAN AND HIS LIFE

- Dan Leno was born as George Wild Galvin into a family of travelling entertainers on 20 December 1860 in Somers Town, London
- He was one of six children and the son of John Galvin and Louisa Dutton

- His father died in 1864 when he was just 37 years old and his mother re-married eighteen months later to Will Leno, a comedian
- His parents appeared on stage under the name of Mr and Mrs Johnny Wild
- He was just 4 years of age when he first appeared on stage as a tumbler and contortionist under the stage name of 'Little George the Infant Wonder Contortionist and Posturer'
- An accident, however, meant that he had to change his act from tumbling to dancing and the singing of comic songs
- In 1880 he won a world championship belt for clog dancing, in a competition that was held in Leeds
- In 1883 he met Sarah Lydia Reynolds and they were married the following year, going on to have six children together
- From 1888 onwards, right up until his death in fact, he appeared in Panto at Drury Lane Theatre. For the rest of the year he played the music halls around the country, building up a reputation as one of the most popular entertainers of his time with an act based on comic songs and monologues; he was also a master at character creation, the most celebrated of which was the immortal Mrs Kelly upon whom he drew to create his equally immortal Panto Dames
- He also appeared in short comedy films
- In 1901 he appeared by Royal Command in front of Edward VII at Sandringham, thus acquiring the nickname 'The King's Jester'
- In 1897 he took his music-hall act to New York, which in those days was considered half way around the world!
- In 1903, and apparently due to the pressures of his fame, he suffered a mental breakdown and was admitted to a mental institution
- Dan Leno died insane on 31 October year 1904. Sadly, and too late, it is now thought it highly likely that a brain tumour was responsible for his increasingly erratic behaviour and eventual death. If only that could have been recognised at the time, when insanity carried such a social stigma
- Crowds lined the streets, at times ten deep, on the day of his funeral – a man and a performer loved by all

## AND FINALLY

- The role of Mother Goose was created specifically for Dan Leno
- For a man, standing a mere 5ft 3in, he was not very tall at all

- He was the pioneer of stand-up comedy and was a great creator of comedic characters through which he delivered many of his routines
- He was an active member of the entertainment charity the Grand Order of Water Rats, which to this day maintains his grave
- His ghost is said to haunt the Theatre Royal, Drury Lane
- Before he was 28 years old, he was the UK's most popular comedian and billed as 'The Funniest Man on Earth'

# DANNY LA RUE OBE

*1927–2009*
*Known as an actor and a 'Comic in a Frock'*

## THE MAN AND HIS LIFE

Breaking with tradition, Danny La Rue was the 'glam' Dame.

- Danny La Rue was born on 26 July 1927 as Daniel Patrick Carroll in Cork, Ireland; he was the youngest in a family of five children
- He moved to England at the age of 9 years and lived for a while in London before being evacuated to Devon during the Second World War
- At the age of 15 years he left school to work in a fashion store in Exeter
- It was when he served for a while in the navy that he learned the joys of the concert parties, thus making him set his sights on a future theatrical career
- He worked in cabaret in many night clubs in London's West End, including Winston's and Churchill's, as well as performing in many stage productions prior to opening his own nightclub – 'Danny La Rue's' –in 1964 in Hanover Square, London
- His nightclub attracted thousands of members as well as celebrities, such as Judy Garland, Shirley Bassey and even royalty of the day
- In 1969 Danny was named as the Variety Club of Great Britain's Showbiz Personality of the Year
- The following year he was named as Theatre Personality of the Year

- After twenty-five years in show business, the Variety Club of Great Britain honoured Danny with a luncheon held in recognition of his services to the world of entertainment
- In 1979 he was proclaimed Entertainer of the Decade
- In 1982 he made theatre history when he opened in Birmingham in the musical *Hello Dolly* playing the part of Dolly Levi. This was the first time that the part of Dolly had been played by a man, as well as being the first time that a man had played a female role in a large musical. (Of course, this has since changed as one of the female leads in the stage musical *Hairspray* is now traditionally played by a man)
- In 1984 Jack Hanson, Danny's partner and manager of forty years, died in New Zealand
- In 1987 Danny La Rue held the title of King Rat in the Grand Order of the Water Rats
- In 2002 Danny La Rue was awarded the OBE in the Queen's Birthday Honours list
- He suffered a mild stroke in 2006
- In 2007 he made an appearance in a musical compilation show entitled *Hello Danny*, in which he played himself at the Benidorm Palace in Spain
- Danny La Rue lost his battle with cancer on 31 May 2009 with his friend and companion Annie Galbraith by his side

## AND FINALLY

- Danny was 'Mr Entertainment' through and through and, like many people in this business we call 'show', he kept 'working' to the end at a job he adored and one that he didn't consider work; Danny La Rue in fact lived and died for his work
- He starred in major West End shows, in film, television and in over fifty Pantos
- In his early years in Panto Danny teamed up many times with Alan Haynes to play the Uglies
- He appeared before the Royal family on no less than thirty occasions
- Danny La Rue always finished his shows as himself, in a suit
- And I just have to finish with a personal comment: Danny La Rue was my late mother's most favourite entertainer of all time and for that reason I had so much pleasure in writing this piece

# DOUGLAS BYNG

*1893–1987*
*He was billed as 'Bawdy but British'*
*'The most refined vulgarity in London', Noel Coward*

## THE MAN AND HIS LIFE

- Douglas Byng was born on 17 March 1893 in Nottinghamshire
- His father was a bank manager and his mother a former school teacher
- At the age of 10 he was sent to live with his older brother in Germany
- He made his first appearance in a Panto in 1921 when he starred in *Aladdin* at the London Palladium
- In 1924 he appeared as Eliza the Cook in *Dick Whittington* at the New Oxford Theatre; this role was later to prove to be one of his most successful and popular Dame roles which he repeated on numerous occasions
- Some critics thought that Byng's humour was too sophisticated for younger audiences and consequently he was banned several times by the BBC
- He was also well known for his ostentatious and outrageous comic costumes, one of which was a fur cape created entirely from bathroom loofahs
- He was a cabaret star too and topped the bill of the famous Cochran Revues, between 1925 and 1931
- During the Second World War he toured widely as a member of ENSA
- In 1971 Douglas Byng appeared on Michael Parkinson's TV show, revitalising his act and introducing him to an entire new audience
- A workaholic, he made his final stage appearance in 1986 at the National in London
- Douglas Byng died on 24 August 1987 in Hillingdon, Middlesex

## AND FINALLY

- Douglas was a prolific writer of comic songs and a master of the double entendre
- He had a very strange and incurable nervous affliction which resulted in his right arm flying suddenly upwards, whilst his head flicked to one side.

Byng did not let this stop his success and so he incorporated it into his act
- He was still appearing on the stage at the grand old age of 90
- Having appeared on the stage for seventy-two years, his was one of the most successful careers in the history of British show business

# FRANCIS LAIDLER

*1867–1954*
*Known as the 'King of Panto'*

## THE MAN AND HIS LIFE

- Francis Laidler was born the son of a doctor in Thornby-on-Tees on 5 January 1867
- He is known and remembered for his association not only with Panto, but with Bradford too where he was first employed as a clerk in the wool trade before going on to work for a local brewery company
- In 1888 Francis married Annie Uthank with whom he went on to have four daughters
- In 1902 Francis went into partnership with Walter Piper, who ran the Prince's Theatre in Bradford, whilst retaining his job at the brewery
- The following year he left the brewery and became full-time manager of the Prince's Theatre, Water Piper having now died
- He soon realised that Panto could pull in the punters and thus increase the revenue of a theatre and so he expanded his theatrical interests and eventually the now famous Alhambra Theatre in Bradford was built
- The Alhambra Theatre, Bradford was opened in 1914
- Annie Laidler died in 1919, leaving Francis Laidler a widower with four daughters
- In 1926 Francis remarried. His second wife, younger than him by almost twenty years, was an actress and was one of the most famous Panto Principal Boys of her time. Her name was Gladwys Stanley – she had changed her usually spelling of the name Gladys to a more theatrical version!
- Whilst conducting his theatrical business and productions in Bradford, Francis famously preferred to live in a suite of rooms at the Great Northern Hotel. He did though own property in London, which Gladwys preferred

- He was soon producing Pantos on a national basis
- On 27 December 1954 Francis Laidler suffered a heart attack and died ten days later on 6 January 1955, just one day before his 88th birthday, which was never-the-less still at a grand old age of 87 years
- After his death, his widow Gladwys continued to run the Laidler theatrical empire
- In March 1957 the widow of Francis Laidler, Gladwys, met her future husband, Frank Woodhead, who was a business man and company director. It was in the same year that the Theatre Royal closed its doors for the last time; a department store was then built on its site
- Gladwys then withdrew from producing and in 1958 the first non-Laidler Panto opened at the Alhambra Theatre in Bradford – a theatrical era had officially come to an end; the Laidler years of Panto had stretched from 1902 until 1958
- Gladwys died in 1978 at the age of 74 years

## AND FINALLY

- It was Francis Laidler who founded the now famous group of Panto Juveniles known as The Sunbeams, which still exist to this day

# JACK TRIPP MBE

*1922–2005*
*Actor, singer, dancer and Panto Dame*
*He was once described by the* Stage *newspaper as the 'John Gielgud of Pantos'*

## THE MAN AND HIS LIFE

- Jack Tripp was born on 4 February 1922 in Plymouth, Devon as the only son of baker William Tripp and his wife Lillian
- He began dancing when he was very young, excelling at tap and became known as the 'Fred Astaire' of Plymouth
- He served in the army during the Second World War
- Whilst in the army he joined the Stars in Battledress Unit, as did many who were later to become successful in the theatrical world during the post-war years

- As well as becoming one of the greatest Panto Dames of all time, he was a well-known variety show and revue artist
- In the 1940s he joined the *Half Past Eight* show in Glasgow where he played alongside Beryl Reid, who was to become his lifelong friend
- He made his West End debut in 1946 when he understudied Sid Field in *Piccadilly Hayride* at the Prince of Wales
- He was the principal comedian in the Fols de Rols seaside summer shows where he stayed for fourteen years
- He first appeared in Panto during the 1940s, when he played alongside Douglas Byng as the Dame's son Billy in *Goody Two Shoes*
- In 1955 he starred alongside Shirley Bassey and Al Read in the revue *Such is Life*
- In the 1960s and 1970s he appeared in his own show, *Take a Trip*, which played various resorts around the UK
- In 1996 he was awarded an MBE for his services to Panto
- He appeared in *Divorce Me, Darling* at Chichester Festival in 1997 with Ruthie Henshall and Tim Flavin
- His final appearance in Panto was in the 1995–6 season in the role Mother Goose in Plymouth
- He finally retired from acting in 2000
- Jack Tripp died at the age of 83 years on 10 July 2005 in Hove, Sussex and was survived by his long-term partner Allen Christie

## AND FINALLY

- Jack Tripp has at least thirty-five Panto Dame credits to his name
- He was renowned for his 'clean' approach to the role of Dame at a time when some performers were introducing a more smutty and crude style
- His costumes were as clean as his characterisation and he is remembered as the Dame who always wore lace-trimmed gingham dresses, bloomers and a snow-white pinny
- He famously declared that '*Mother Goose* is the *Hamlet* of Pantos'

# JEFFREY HOLLAND

*1946–*
*The actor renowned for his eternal boyish looks and gentlemanly ways*

## THE MAN AND HIS LIFE

- Jeffrey Holland was born Jeffrey Parkes on 17 July 1946 in Walsall, the son of Samuel and Doris Parkes. He has one brother, Steven, and was educated at Queen Mary's Grammar School
- The acting bug bit him when he was in his teens and at the age of 19 he became a member of the Minster Players Amateur Dramatic Society
- After deciding to become a professional actor, he went on to train at the Birmingham School of Speech Training and Dramatic Art
- He made his professional debut at the Alexandra Theatre, Birmingham in 1967 as Frank Mullins, the Judge's Clerk, in Henry Cecil's play *No Fear Or Favour*
- In 1971 Jeffrey Holland married his first wife, actress Eleanor Hartopp, with whom he went on to have two children, a daughter, Lucy, and a son, Sam
- In 1975 he was a part of the cast of the musical stage version of *Dad's Army*
- His introduction into the world of Panto Dames came in 1989 when he volunteered to play the Dame in a new production of *Sleeping Beauty* at the Theatre Royal, Plymouth. The show was starring Hinge and Bracket as the Witch and the Fairy and no one would accept the role of Dame alongside two other 'drag' acts. Having already been engaged to play the Comic, Jeffrey uttered the fatal three words 'I'll do it!' He did and has never looked back since
- In 2004 Jeffrey Holland married his second wife, Judy Buxton
- 2012 saw him cast in the film version of Ray Cooney's farce *Run for Your Wife*

## AND FINALLY

- Jeffrey Holland is now a Panto veteran having appeared in well over forty Pantos over the years, putting him in the top five of currently playing Dames
- Although now recognised as one of the country's top Dames, Jeffrey is also a well-renowned TV performer having played hugely memorable roles in such sitcoms as *Dad's Army*, *It Ain't Half Hot, Mum!* and *Are You Being Served?*, but is mainly known for, *Oh, Dr Beeching!*, *You Rang, M'Lord?* and *Hi de Hi!*, the last of which turned him into a household name. In addition, he has played a variety of roles in productions ranging from *Coronation Street* to *Henry V*
- Jeffrey is also a huge fan of *Star Trek* and Laurel and Hardy
- It is interesting to note that wherever I turned for research on Jeffrey Holland I was met with the words: 'Jeffrey Holland? Oh such a lovely guy!'

## JOE PASQUALE

*1961–*
*The man with the squeaky voice who has also been crowned the 'King of the Jungle'*

## THE MAN AND HIS LIFE

- Joe Pasquale was born on 20 August 1961 in Grays, Essex as Joseph Ellis Pasquale
- In 1978 he married Alison with whom he went on to have three children before their divorce in 1986
- Before becoming a professional entertainer Joe worked in the Civil Service's Department of Transport, Smithfields Meat Market and the Ford Factory in Dagenham, Essex
- Like many comedians before him, Joe then went on to learn his craft on the holiday camp circuit
- In 1987 Joe got his big break when he came second in the TV talent show *New Faces*
- He married his second wife, Debbie, in 1988

- In 1999 Joe Pasquale turned his hand to acting for the very first time when he toured for twelve weeks in the lead role of the critically acclaimed play *The Nerd*
- In 2001 Joe Pasquale was the only British performer to be invited to appear in an American TV show celebrating the twenty-fifth anniversary of the *Muppet Show*
- In 2004 he was crowned 'King of the Jungle' when he took part in the TV reality show *I'm a Celebrity, Get Me Out of Here*
- In 2005 he stretched his acting wings even further when he starred in a film playing the part of the Pink Lieutenant in *Dead Long Enough*
- In 2005 Joe ran the Virgin London Marathon to raise money for Diabetes UK
- In 2008 he split from Debbie, his wife of twenty years; they had two children together
- In 2013 Joe took part in the TV series *Dancing on Ice*, where he was partnered by Vicky Ogden

## AND FINALLY

- We may think of him as the funny bloke with the squeaky voice but he is in fact a very accomplished actor – both comedic and straight
- He is also a qualified pilot and is currently studying for a degree in geoscience
- His son Joe is also an actor and has appeared in the Channel 4 soap opera *Hollyoaks*
- Joe Pasquale, the comedian with brains, appeared on *Celebrity Mastermind* and scored 17 out of 17 on his specialist subject 'Vampires in the Cinema from 1896 to the present day', but in his own words was s**t at the general knowledge questions and only managed to get five correct answers

# JOHN INMAN

*1935–2007*
*Well known for his catch phrase 'I'm free'*

## THE MAN AND HIS LIFE

- John Inman was born as Frederick John Inman on 28 June 1935 in Preston, Lancashire, the son of two hairdressers

- Before he hit his teens he moved with his parents to Blackpool, where they opened a boarding house
- One could say his road to professionalism began when his parents paid for him to have elocution lessons at a time when a regional accent was considered a handicap in the world of theatre
- He made his stage debut on Blackpool's famous South Pier when he was just 13 years old
- He began his working life in the retail industry – ironic, as it was his role as Mr Humphries in the sitcom *Are You Being Served?* which brought him his later international fame
- Aged 17 years he moved to London to continue his career in the retail industry – as a window dresser
- He lived in a bedsit in London and topped up his income by sewing garments for the London theatres
- He also worked as a scenic artist in order to gain his Equity Card at a time when a card was needed to work professionally
- Having attained his Equity Card he worked professionally in a number of productions
- His West End debut was in the musical *Ann Veronica* at the Cambridge Theatre; this was followed by a stint as Lord Fancourt Babberley in *Charley's Aunt* at the Adelphi Theatre
- In 1972 his big break came when he landed the role of the camp Mr Humphries in the new TV sitcom *Are You Being Served?*, a role he was to play until the mid-1980s when the show finally came off air
- In 1977 ITV offered him an exclusive contract and his own show called *Odd Man Out*. Sadly, though, the show was not a success and ran for only seven episodes
- The final episode of *Are You Being Served* aired in 1985
- In the later years of his life John Inman was plagued by ill health – in 1993 he collapsed at home suffering from bronchitis and was taken to hospital; in 1995 he collapsed during a performance of *Mother Goose*; in 2004 he had to withdraw from *Dick Whittington* at the Richmond Theatre after contracting the liver disease hepatitis A, which he apparently contracted through eating contaminated food
- In December 2005 John Inman and his partner of more than thirty years, Ron Lynch, entered into a civil partnership
- He worked tirelessly for charitable causes over the years
- John Inman died on 8 March 2007 aged 71 years

## AND FINALLY

- John worked endlessly for charity and is a past King Rat of the Grand Order of Water Rats
- The role of Mr Humphries won him the BBC's Personality of the Year Award
- He was an accomplished golfer, with an handicap of three
- During his lifetime he became one of the UK's best-loved Dames, appearing in over forty Pantos during his lifetime, often alternating the Christmas Panto season with the summer show season – the latter being another of his loves

# LES DAWSON

*1934–93*
*The man with the rubber face!*

## THE MAN AND HIS LIFE

- Les Dawson was born on 2 February 1934 in Collyhurst, Manchester; he was an only child
- His father was a bricklayer
- His first job was in the parcels department of the Manchester Co-op
- He also spent a short time on the *Bury Times* from where he was given the sack after submitting an inappropriate funeral report. But not because, as one would expect, it was an insensitive report, but because it was too literary in approach, beginning with the words: 'On a rain-swept plateau the mourners huddled together as the cold, grey mist embraced them in its clammy shroud'
- Whilst waiting to establish himself as a comedian he had a variety of jobs from selling vacuum cleaners to washing dishes
- He worked the northern club scene trying to establish himself
- The act that emerged from his practical apprenticeship was unique in that it was a miserable act from a miserable-looking slob who became renowned for his mother-in-law jokes! His delivery was often verbose and, some would say even misogynist in approach
- In 1959 he married Margaret (Meg) Plant with whom he went on to have one son and two daughters. She was later to leave him a widower after an eight-year battle with cancer

- It was in 1967 and at the age of 36 that he won the TV talent show *Opportunity Knocks*
- He later went on to be a huge success as host of another TV show called *Blankety Blank*
- In 1989 he married Tracy Roper and together they had one daughter, Charlotte
- Les Dawson died of a heart attack on 10 June 1993. He died in hospital where ironically he had gone for a check-up. It was his third and final heart attack that killed him; his daughter, Charlotte, was just 8 months old at the time

## AND FINALLY

- Les Dawson was also a writer with a dozen books to his credit and a personal library of 4,000 books
- He was an excellent linguist too for he spoke Japanese, French, German and Italian
- His nickname as a child was Dossy
- For comedic effect, he played the piano very badly, which my husband – himself a musician – tells me for someone musical is much harder than playing it well
- On 23 October 2008, fifteen years after his death, a bronze statue of Les Dawson, by sculptor Graham Ibbeson, was unveiled by his widow Tracy and daughter Charlotte in St Anne's-on-Sea, Lancashire
- And his view of himself? He always said that he was: 'A fat man with a face like a collapsed sponge cake' – Oh no, Mr Dawson, you were so much more than that!

# PAUL O'GRADY MBE

*1955–*
*Well known for his drag queen creation Lily Savage*

## THE MAN AND HIS LIFE

- Paul O'Grady was born as Paul James Michael O'Grady on 14 June 1955 in Birkenhead to Patrick (Paddy) Grady and Mary Savage
- His family was of Irish descent

- He was a pupil at Christian Brothers School and after leaving school worked for a while as a clerk in a magistrates' office
- In 1973 Paul's father passed away
- At this time in his life he met Diane Jansen with whom he had a brief relationship resulting in the birth of his daughter, Sharyn, in 1974
- Paul decided that he was too young for fatherhood and so travelled Europe instead
- After he left school he travelled around the country trying his hand at several jobs, jobs such as civil service and bar work
- In 1977 he married Theresa Fernandes
- In the 1980s he created his now infamous drag act character, Lily Savage, and it was 'she' who was to be the key to success he has enjoyed since
- In 1988, when he was 33, Paul's beloved mother passed away
- His success as an entertainer grew and he went on to present shows such as *Blankety Blank* and *Lily Live*
- In 2000 he retired Lily and began to make appearances as himself, Paul O'Grady
- In 2000 he suffered a heart attack since which he has led a calm and more relaxing life on a farm in the south of England, with his beloved animals
- In 2005 Paul and Theresa divorced; in the same year he was given an honorary fellowship to Liverpool John Moores University
- In 2005 his long-term lover and business partner of twenty years, Brendan Murphy, died
- He won a BAFTA for his *New Paul O'Grady Show* in 2005
- Courtesy of his daughter, Sharyn, to whom he is very close, and son-in-law, Philip, in 2006 Paul became a grandfather for the first time when Sharyn gave birth to her first child, a son whom she called Abel Moseley
- In 2008 he was awarded an MBE for his services to entertainment

## AND FINALLY

- He stands an imposing 6ft in height
- A great animal lover, three of Paul's dogs, Buster, Olga and Louie are almost as famous as Paul himself, having appeared regularly with him on his tea-time TV show

# MELVYN HAYES MBE

*1935–*
*The little chap with the huge CV*

## THE MAN AND HIS LIFE

- Melvyn Hayes was born on 11 January 1935 as Melvyn Hyams. He was born in London within the sound of Bow Bells, which means that he is a true Cockney
- In 1939, the year of the outbreak of the Second World War, Melvyn was evacuated to Devon with his two older brothers; he was just 4½ years old at the time and his brothers were 9 and 13
- He returned to London when he was about 8 or 9 years old; it was at the time when the sound of the overhead doodlebugs terrorised Londoners, a sound that he vividly remembers to this day.
- He was educated at Sir Walter St John's Grammar School, Battersea, London
- After leaving school, and tired of constant comments that he should be a jockey as he was so small, he joined a racing stables in Epsom, Surrey. Unhappy though, he lasted just two weeks at the stables
- His next job was as a messenger boy in Fleet Street, London
- It was whilst on this job that he saw an advert in the *Daily Mirror* for an agile and diminutive actor to perform the Indian Rope Trick; qualifying on two out of three counts, he applied and got the job!
- Melvyn's professional career began then in 1950 at the Comedy Theatre, London
- He went on, as many actors of the time, to learn his craft in the theatre repertory companies
- His career went from strength to strength with appearances on both the small and large screen, in addition to his theatre and radio work
- In 1957 he gave one of his most memorable performances as Edek, in the children's television production of *The Silver Sword*, the story about

Polish refugee children trying to find their parents after the Second World War

- Melvyn Hayes has six children by his three wives
- In 1962 he married his first wife, Rosalind Allen, with whom he went on to have three children
- In 1974 he married his second wife, Wendy Padbury, and together they had two daughters
- In 1980, whilst playing the London Palladium, Melvyn Hayes was the surprise subject of Thames Television's *This is Your Life*
- In 2010 he married his third, and current, wife, Jayne Male, with whom he has one child
- It was in the 1970s that he landed the part of Gunner (later Bombardier) Gloria Beaumont in the TV sitcom *It Aint Half Hot Mum*. The show ran for seven years
- In the 1990s Melvyn and Jayne began fostering children, which they continue to do and more than forty children in need of a loving home having crossed their threshold to date
- In 2005 Melvyn held the position of King Rat of the Grand Order of Water Rats
- In 2010 Melvyn Hayes helped raise £200,000 to reopen a burned-out theatre in Long Eaton, Derbyshire

## AND FINALLY

- Melvyn is 5ft 3in tall
- His daughter, Charlie Hayes, has followed him into the business and is an actress
- A second daughter, Talla Gittens, runs a theatre school, Beginners on Stage, together with an agency in Hampshire, another arm of the entertainment world in the hands of a Hayes family member
- He appeared in three Cliff Richard films, *The Young Ones*, *Summer Holiday* and *Wonderful Life*
- He was the voice of Bob Cratchitt in a cartoon film of *A Christmas Carol* which won an Oscar for Best Cartoon Film
- He has appeared in more than fifty films, a dozen West End productions, British and overseas provincial tours, 500 TV shows, as well as radio shows, summer seasons and, of course, Pantos. In fact, the list goes on

and on and if it's a part of the entertainment business, then Melvyn has been a part of 'it'!

- And the last word goes to Melvyn: 'When I started, it was Joe Public sitting at home being entertained by professionals. Now it's out-of-work professionals sitting at home being entertained by Joe Public!'

# NIGEL ELLACOTT

*1953–*
*Panto actor and writer, he is the Dame who lives and dreams Panto; he is Panto!*

## THE MAN AND HIS LIFE

- Nigel Ellacott was born on 28 February 1953 in Swansea, South Wales where he also grew up
- Nigel's older brother is the celebrated Vivyan Ellacott who has also spent a lifetime in theatre as a director and theatre manager
- After appearing in Pantos in various guises, including three times as geese (*Mother Goose*), twice as *Puss in Boots* and other assorted characters, from 1974, Nigel first appeared in *Cinderella* with his stage partner, Peter Robbins, in 1981 at the Kenneth More Theatre, Ilford
- It was in 1983 that Nigel and Peter began their association with Paul Elliott's E. & B. Productions and it was for them that they went on to play the Ugly Sisters in *Cinderella* in numerous theatres around the country
- In 1996 E. & B. Productions suggested to Nigel and Peter that they take their show out to schools and introduce the next generation to this very special form of theatre – and so the *Panto Roadshow* was born where children learned a little about the history of Panto as well as, with the hands-on approach, being allowed to dress up and join in! To date this show has played to over 80,000 children nationwide

- In 1997 Nigel and Peter were featured in Channel 4's documentary *Pantoland*, which was later repeated in 1999
- In 2003 Nigel and his 'sister' Peter were asked to be the face of the Royal Mail Post Office's Christmas advertising campaign with their image as the 'Sisters' appearing as life-sized cut-outs, on banners and posters in every Post Office throughout the country
- On 15 April 2009, Peter Robbins tragically died very suddenly, bringing to an end a partnership that had lasted almost thirty years
- The Panto season of 2009/10 arrived and after the early death of his professional partner, Peter Robbins, Nigel made his first solo Dame performance as Dolly Doughnut in *Snow White* when he returned to the theatre where he ironically began his 'Sister' career with Peter way back in 1981

## AND FINALLY

- Nigel has written more than twenty-six Panto scripts, all of which have been produced throughout the UK as well as three in America
- Each year for the past thirty years he has designed costumes for Pantos across the country
- Panto is not a seasonal event for Nigel, but a year-long way of life as he travels the country introducing both young and old alike to the joys of this very special British tradition
- As well as creating and hosting the largest website all about Panto – www.its-behind-you.com – Nigel is generous with his expertise and knowledge about his special world and is always willing to share this with anyone who cares to ask
- This man has dedicated his professional life exclusively to the art of Pantomime, for which the industry and art form has much to be grateful
- This is the man who not only gives to the art every single Christmas, but every single year in its entirety

Nigel's impressive credits as one half of the Uglies in *Cinderella* include:

| 1981 | Kenneth More Theatre, Ilford | featuring | Chris Lloyd, John Griffiiths, Gareth Snook |
| 1982 | Grand Pavilion, Porthcawl | featuring | Ria Jones, Neil West, Bryn Williams |
| 1983 | Gordon Craig Theatre, Stevenage | featuring | Peter Byrne, Katherine Apanowitz, Linda Hayden |
| 1984 | Beck Theatre, Hayes | featuring | Dennis Waterman, Rula Lenska, Peter Purves |
| 1985 | Pavilion Theatre, Bournemouth | featuring | Rolf Harris, Kathy Staff, Bill Owen |
| 1986 | Richmond Theatre | featuring | Rolf Harris, Anneka Rice, Bill Owen |
| 1987 | His Majesty's, Aberdeen | featuring | Bill Owen, Paul Henry, Fiona Kennedy |
| 1988 | Mayflower, Southampton | featuring | Paul Nicholas, Roy Walker, Dame Hilda Bracket |
| 1989 | New Theatre, Hull | featuring | Les Dennis, Ronnie Hilton, Sophie Alred |
| 1990 | New Theatre, Cardiff | featuring | Jonathon Morris, Windsor Davies, Dame Hilda |
| 1991 | Grand Theatre, Leeds | Transfer | Transferred from New Theatre, Cardiff |
| 1991 | Ashcroft, Croydon | featuring | June Brown, Windsor Davies, Andrew O'Connor |
| 1992 | Pavilion Theatre, Bournemouth | featuring | Stefan Denis, June Brown, Windsor Davies |
| 1993 | Lyceum, Sheffield | featuring | Cannon and Ball, Polly Perkins, Caroline Dennis |
| 1994 | Wimbledon Theatre | featuring | Rolf Harris, June Whitfield, Mark Curry |
| 1995 | Hippodrome, Birmingham | featuring | Gary Wilmot, Rolf Harris, Judy Cornwell, Robin Cousins, Jodie Jackson, Bob Carolgees |
| 1996 | Victoria Theatre, Woking | featuring | Gary Wilmot, Rolf Harris, Judy Cornwell, Robin Cousins, Jodie Jackson, Bob Carolgees |
| 1997 | Theatre Royal, Nottingham | featuring | Bradley Walsh, Judy Cornwell, Peter Baldwin |
| 1998 | Wimbledon Theatre | featuring | Bradley Walsh, Britt Ekland, Kris Akabusi |
| 1999 | Kings, Edinburgh | featuring | Dorothy Paul, Allan Stewart, Andy Gray |
| 2000 | Civic Theatre, Darlington | featuring | Ray Meagher, Stu Francis, Judy Buxton |
| 2001 | Her Majesty's, Aberdeen | featuring | Jansen Spence, Stu Francis, Billy Riddoch |
| 2002 | Mayflower Southampton | featuring | Brian Conley, Dawson Chance, Lynsey Britten, Rachel Spry |

| 2003 | Opera House, Manchester | featuring | Brian Conley, Dawson Chance, Lynsey Britten, Rachel Spry |
|------|------|------|------|
| 2004 | Theatre Royal, Plymouth | featuring | Brian Conley, Dawson Chance, Lynsey Britten, Sean Needham, Rachel Spry, Jody Crosier |
| 2005 | Theatre Royal, Newcastle upon Tyne | featuring | Jill Halfpenny, Clive Webb, Danny Adams, Sean Needham, Jody Crosier, Lauren Hill, Emma Katy Adcock, Amy Burns, Amy Bruce, Jenny Dougan, Innis Robertson, Sean Hackett, Karl Williams, Ricardo Canadinhas, Marron Stage School |
| 2006 | Hippodrome, Birmingham | featuring | Brian Conley, Shobna Gulati, Dawson Chance, Sean Needham, Jody Crosier, Michelle Potter, Sinead Blairs, Louise Corbett, Nathan Daniel, Sean Hackett, Lucy James, Bethany King, Desi Valentine, Wesley Wareham, Kitty Whitelaw, Andy Young |
| 2007 | Wycombe Swan, High Wycombe | featuring | Brian Conley, Dawson Chance, Jody Crosier, Michelle Potter, Dean Chisnall, Kerry Winter, Rossana Stocchino, Philip Dzwonkiewicz, Lia Given, Lucy Harrison, Sarah Riches, Jack Jefferson |
| 2008 | Theatre Royal, Nottingham | featuring | Brian Conley, Dawson Chance, Michelle Potter, Denise Pitter, Dean Chisnall, Eaton James, Toby James Anderson, Lorna Bullivant, Gemma Formaston, Aaron Sweeney Harris, Sergio Giacomelli, Nathan Holliday, Jessica Hosken, Hayley Ellen Scott |

# PETER ROBBINS

*31 March 1953–15 April 2009*
*Peter Robbins' death meant that these Uglies could be no more, thus creating a huge void in the world of Panto; a void that will never be filled after the death of a man who will never be forgotten*

Nigel continued his career in Panto – flying solo:

| 2009 | Kenneth More Theatre, Ilford | featuring | Isobel Hurll, Loraine Porter, Michael Conway, (*Snow White*) Ellie Robertson, Rikki Stone, Robert Quarry, Tami Stone, Jocelyn Prah, Owen Smith, Nathan Daniel |
| 2010 | Orchard Theatre, Dartford | featuring | Bobby Davro, Wayne Perrey and Jay Worthy (*Jack and the Beanstalk*) |
| 2011 | Venue Cymru, Llandudno | featuring | Lucy May Barker, John Evans, Jason Gardiner, Tim (*Aladdin*) Morgan, Marc Mulcahey, Rebecca Parker |
| 2012 | Grand Theatre, Wolverhampton | featuring | Niki Evans, Keith Harris (with Orville and Cuddles), (*Jack and the Beanstalk*) Sherrie Hewson, Ben James-Ellis, Ken Morley |

# NORMAN EVANS

*1901–62*
*Known and loved for his 'Over the Garden Wall' sketch*

## THE MAN AND HIS LIFE

- Norman Evans was born on 11 June 1901 in Rochdale, Lancashire, the son of a Rochdale organist
- He was educated at Castlemere Council School in Rochdale
- His first job after leaving school was as an office boy in a Lancashire mill, where he earned a mere 25p (5*s* in 'old' money) a week
- He then had a variety of jobs which included working as a salesman and an insurance agent before he realised his destiny was to be an entertainer
- Before turning professional, he was a prominent member of the Rochdale Amateur Dramatic Society
- In 1931 he was discovered by another Rochdale performer, the great comedienne and singer Gracie Fields, when she topped the bill at a charity show at the Rochdale Hippodrome; so impressed was she by Norman, who was appearing on the same bill, that she suggested he turned professional
- Gracie took the then unknown Norman Evans under her wing and in 1934 she selflessly cut 20 minutes out of her own act at the Chiswick Empire to give him a taste of professional variety

- In 1934 Norman's wife, Annie, gave birth to their only child, a daughter, Norma
- In 1936 Norman first appeared in a Royal Variety Show
- Norman's greatest love soon became playing the Dame in Panto and in 1937 Bernard Beard, the manager of Keighley Hippodrome, said he had never heard such laughter in a variety theatre and telephoned the renowned Francis Laidler to tell him so!
- There soon followed an invitation from Francis Laidler to play the Dame in *Aladdin* at the Prince's Theatre in Bristol
- In 1944/5 he starred in the longest running Panto ever, *Humpty Dumpty*, at the Leeds Theatre Royal. The Panto ran for a record twenty-two weeks, a record that is now highly unlikely ever to be broken
- In 1947 Norman made his second appearance in a Royal Variety Show
- In 1949 he crossed the pond to appear in New York on the Ed Sullivan Show
- In the UK he then toured with his own revue show, *Good Evans*, in which he introduced his daughter as a vocalist
- In 1951 Norman made his third appearance in a Royal Variety Show
- In 1955 he was seriously injured in a car accident in which he lost his left eye
- Norman Evans kept on working right up until his death on 25 November 1962

## AND FINALLY

- Before becoming an entertainer, he was for many years a lay preacher
- He is, to date, the only Panto Dame to be given top billing at the London Palladium
- Norman created the rubber-faced character called Fanny Fairbrother, a toothless woman known for gossiping over the fence, who was later to be the inspiration for Les Dawson's rubber-faced gossip
- On 8 August 1999 he was honoured posthumously with the unveiling of a plaque at the Manchester Opera House
- He appeared in several television shows and films
- The headstone on his grave is a low wall and the inscription reads: 'Norman's last garden wall!'

# SIR NORMAN WISDOM

*1915–2010*
*The lovable fool*
*'Don't Laugh at Me 'Cause I'm a Fool'* – *signature song*

## THE MAN AND HIS LIFE

- Norman Joseph Wisdom was born into poverty in London on 4 February 1915, the second son of Frederick and Maud Wisdom
- His was a poor and violent family life which often saw him walk to school barefoot
- After his mother left the family home, Norman and his brother were placed in a children's home
- He left school at the age of 14 years and, disowned by his father, he was forced to sleep rough
- In 1941 he married Doreen Brett and together they had one son, Michael, who was born in 1945. The marriage ended in divorce
- At the outbreak of the Second World War he joined the army, aged 24 years, where he served in India and learned the skills of boxing
- After numerous jobs, his break in the entertainment industry came in 1945 at the Collins Hall, Islington, a venue for new variety turns where he was able to show audiences his unique slapstick and knock-about humour. Billed as 'The Successful Failure', he played the fool and audiences loved him for it
- It was in 1947 that Norman Wisdom married his second wife, Freda Simpson, with whom he had another two children, Nicholas, born in 1953, and Jacqueline, born in 1954; this marriage also ended in divorce and Norman Wisdom was granted custody of both children
- In 1952 he made his first appearance on a Royal Variety Show and later went on to appear in another eight
- It was in the 1950s that Norman Wisdom, along with that other veteran of the stage, Bruce Forsthye, appeared on *Sunday Night at the London Palladium* as a duo to perform the classic Panto sketch of 'Papering the Parlour'. This is a sketch many try but few succeed with the expert and professional timing of these two great comedians
- He appeared as Aladdin at the London Palladium in 1956 in a sell-out production

- In 1964 a record 18.5 million people watched his BBC Panto *Robinson Crusoe*
- In 1980 he moved to the Isle of Man
- In 1981 he played a terminally ill cancer patient, unable to come to terms with his fate, in the BBC play *Going Gently* for which he won a BAFTA
- In 1995 he was awarded an OBE
- He was knighted in 2000
- At the age of 90 years he announced his long overdue retirement from the entertainment industry – why? Because he wanted to play more golf!
- In 2007 he entered residential care at a nursing home on his beloved Isle of Man – the island he loved so much
- On 4 October 2010 the great comic entertainer/performer that was Norman Wisdom died at the Abbotswood Nursing Home on the Isle of Man. He was 95 years old and had suffered a series of strokes in the six months prior to his death

## AND FINALLY

- Norman Wisdom's signature move, as it is now sometimes called, was his walking trip; though always expected, indeed anticipated, whenever it happened it, it never failed to raise a laugh
- Norman Wisdom is credited with the responsibility for the current trend of the Principal Boy being played by a male actor instead of the customary female actress
- He starred in no less than nineteen movies
- Norman Wisdom was a football and golf enthusiast, as well as a car fanatic
- He could play an amazing eleven musical instruments
- Norman Wisdom did not use a stuntman, but instead performed all of his own stunts
- A favourite with the Royal Family, he was invited to perform for them at Windsor Castle
- He found what was to become his entertainment uniform in a Scarborough charity shop in the guise of a jacket three sizes too small with tie awry and cap askew. This was then his trademark for the rest of his career; he was the eternal schoolboy with the looks of a beaten puppy – and we loved him for it!

- And so it was that Norman Wisdom had a signature tune, 'Don't Laugh at Me 'Cause I'm a Fool', a signature walk which involved an 'expected' trip, and ill-fitting clothes which made him look like an eternal schoolboy.

# ROY HUDD OBE

*1936–*
*Comedian, TV, radio and stage actor*
*Authority on Panto and music-hall entertainment*

## THE MAN AND HIS LIFE

- Roy Hudd was born on 16 May 1936 in Croydon, the son of carpenter and joiner Harry Hudd
- During the Second World War Roy and his family were evacuated to the village of Maidford in Northamptonshire where he went to a local school
- In 1942 Roy's younger brother, Peter, arrived into a world at war
- When Roy was just 7 years old his mother, Evalina – though always called Evie for short – committed suicide and as a consequence Roy was brought up by his grandmother, Alice, whilst his younger brother (by six years), Peter, was brought up by an aunt and uncle. It took him a long time to piece together his own personal story, which in fact was never actually completed until he was researching for his autobiography, *A Fart in a Colander*
- At the end of the war Roy's father, Harry Hudd, left the family home
- Although Roy passed his 11 plus, instead of going to a grammar school he chose Tavistock Secondary Modern School until he could go on to Croydon Secondary Technical School where he could learn a trade – he and his gran thought it best he acquired a trade; although not going to grammar school was a decision he lived to regret
- In 1955 Roy began his national service in the RAF – preferring the colour of the uniform to that of the army and navy!
- In 1958, like many before him and after him, Roy undertook a practical training in entertainment on the job, as it were, when he became a Red Coat at Butlins Holiday Camp, Clacton
- It was in the 1950s that he also played seasons at Richmond Theatre, the Young Vic and Regents Park

- Shakespeare is not a playwright one would expect to say in the same sentence as Roy Hudd and yet in 1960 Roy played Young Gobbo in *The Merchant of Venice* at Richmond; he followed this the next year by playing Sir Andrew Aguecheek in *Twelfth Night*
- In the 1960s Roy Hudd also became famous for his TV shows, *The Illustrated Weekly Hudd* and *The Roy Hudd Show*
- In May 1961 he married his first wife, Ann Lambert
- In July 1964 Roy and Ann's son, Max – or to give him his full title Maxwell Roy – was born.
- In 1980 he starred as Fagin in the musical *Oliver*, a part he reprised in Canada three years later
- In 1988 he married his second wife, Debbie Flitcroft, herself now a force to be reckoned with as a director and choreographer in the land of Panto
- Since the year 2002, Roy keeps popping up every so often in the TV soap *Coronation Street*, when he plays the part of Archie Shuttleworth
- In 2004 Roy Hudd was awarded an OBE in the New Year Honours List for services to entertainment
- In 2009 his autobiography, *A Fart in a Colander*, was published by Michael O' Mara Books Ltd; the title came about because as a child he could never sit still and that was what his grandmother called him!
- In 2007 he was made a Honorary Doctor of Civil Law at the University of East Anglia and 2010 saw him awarded the Honorary Degree of Doctor of Letters by the University of Westminster

## AND FINALLY

- Roy was introduced to the world of theatre and encouraged to follow a career in entertainment by his beloved grandmother when she took him on weekly visits to the Croydon Empire – for a good laugh – and, of course, to see the annual Christmas Panto
- The first Panto he ever saw, he believes, must have been *Dick Whittington* because for two weeks after that trip to the theatre he insisted that all his food – and saucers of milk – were put on the floor for him; clearly the Cat had made a huge impression on him. His grandmother merely complied with his request as though nothing untoward was taking place
- Roy Hudd is widely considered to be a world authority on Panto and music hall and is President of the British Music Hall Society

- He is also known for his charitable works and is a past King Rat of the Grand Order of the Water Rats – twice! He is also a member of the Charities Committee of the Grand Order of Water Rats
- Arthur Askey was once offered the *Sleeping Beauty* Panto at Wimbledon and he said: 'Yes, I'll do it, but I must have Roy Hudd, we work marvellously well together.' It was a lie because they had never even met, but Arthur Askey knew that he had hit a rocky patch and was having a hard time. Danny La Rue was also kind to him at that time when he put him in his review *Danny at the Palace*, on Shaftesbury Avenue, insisting that Roy's name was in lights alongside his at the theatre. This is the Brotherhood of Entertainment at its very best
- Since those lean times, Roy Hudd has appeared in, and written, more than thirty Pantos

## SEB CRAIG

*1937–*
*Actor, comedian, Panto Dame – and a born romantic!*

### THE MAN AND HIS LIFE

- Seb Craig was born in 1937 as Robin Jace Craig, in Coulsdon, Surrey, later changing his name when entering the world of entertainment to Seb Craig
- He was the third son of John Neilson Craig, a bank manager, and Katie Elaine Craig
- Seb was educated at St Faith's and The Leys School, Cambridge and after leaving school he spent two years doing his national service in the Royal Artillery, where he reached the non-commissioned rank of bombardier
- After he was demobbed he won a place at the Central School of Speech and Drama at the Embassy Theatre, London where he studied stage management
- Twelve months later he was offered a job with Leatherhead Repertory Company under the direction of Hazel Vincent Wallace

- Eight weeks later the theatre closed for a summer break and Seb moved to Hornchurch Repertory Theatre. It was 1959 and when he arrived he was introduced to a young student by the name of Rita Buckley, little knowing then that he had just been introduced to his future wife!
- Time passed and the pair became, as we say today, an item before Rita was offered a place at the world-renowned Royal Academy of Dramatic Art (RADA) in London
- In true romantic fashion, Seb followed the love of his life to the big city
- There followed jobs at the Metropolitan Theatre on Edgeware Road before he joined a theatre company in Tunbridge Wells
- In 1959 Seb signed to the agent Vincent Shaw, and has remained with them all these years, through to the end of Vincent's life and beyond (the agency is now called VSA Ltd). A rare testament these day's to one man's loyalty and an agent's ability
- In 1962 there followed work in Eastbourne where he appeared in the premiere of *Love in Bloom* with his now wife, Rita
- Seb and Rita went on to have two children; Carrie, who was born in 1965 and went into the acting profession, and Marc, born in 1968 and who inherited his mother's musical genes and grew to be a gifted musician
- Between the years 1965 and 1973 Seb spent his career as a successful artistic director in various theatres across the UK
- In 1973 he was appointed artistic director of the Shrewsbury Music Hall in Shropshire
- It was here that he wrote and directed seven Pantos, appearing as Dame in three of them
- In 1979 he devised and directed the First British International Song Contest with 970 entries from 32 countries. On the penultimate night there was a concert compèred by Norman Vaughan, starring Frankie Vaughan and Francis Lai who conducted the orchestra with his Oscar-winning arrangement of *Love Story*. Seb's beloved Rita sang 'What I did for Love'
- In 1985 he played Professor Higgins in a short season and sell-out run of *My Fair Lady*
- In 1986 he moved to London and was immediately booked to understudy Frankie Howerd in *A Funny Thing Happened on the Way to the Forum* at the Piccadilly Theatre, London
- In 1989 6ft 4in Seb compèred a national tour of the *Ronnie Corbett Show*

- 1990/1 he appeared in Aykbourn's *Man of the Moment* at the Gielgud
- In 1998 he played Mr Banstread in *Duck Patrol* for ITV with Richard Wilson and David Tennant
- In 2001/2 he appeared in Ray Cooney's *Caught in the Net* at the Vauderville Theatre, London
- In 2005 he appeared in Shakespeare's *Julius Caesar* at the Barbican
- And all the time during his straight/comedy theatre work he also managed, whenever possible, to appear as a Panto Dame around the country, with Rita as his dresser – she happily walking in his shadow
- In November 2005, two hours after their forty-third wedding anniversary, Seb lost his dearly loved wife, his best friend and his personal dresser to cancer
- In 2013 there is still no sign of this bundle of energy slowing down as he appears in two hugely successful TV shows, *That Hidden Camera Family* on SKY 1 and as the lovable tall, skinny character in the hit ITV programme *Off Their Rockers*

## AND FINALLY

- Seb always designed his own Dame costumes, which were then made for him by Pat Moss of Pat Moss Costumes, Shoreham; his wigs were made by Derek Easton; Seb is still the proud owner of all his costumes and wigs
- When Seb lost Rita he appeared to lose his desire to do another Panto. Rita was always his dresser and could change him completely in sixteen bars of music! No one has been able to do that since
- He has been involved in thirty-three Pantomimes and has played Dame on seventeen occasions
- He has also appeared as the lead or featured role in more than seventy commercials worldwide
- And on a personal note it was Seb Craig who first gave my husband, Gwyn, and I our first break in the world of entertainment, for which I will be eternally grateful

*Chapter 5*

# GREAT NAMES IN THE WORLD OF PANTOMIME

The world has, within it, various other worlds of expertise so that we may each enjoy whatever art or science pulls us towards it. It doesn't matter what that world is, and there is nothing that annoys me more than when one person is criticised by another because they do not appreciate the same pass-times. That is a nonsense, an insult and ridiculous. Be it lace making, athletics, stamp collecting, science – whatever – it really does not matter at all; each to his own and horses for courses, I say, and of course we can all learn from others and be introduced to new exciting worlds to explore. I am, of course, talking here about leisure activities and not about medical science, for example. For those worlds demand not acceptance but respect, for which the majority do not require cajoling.

So, back to how we choose to spend our leisure time and more specifically, back to the world of Panto where some of us like to amble along, often as an extension to the thespian world in general. Here, in Panto Land, we have many great names and as has happened in previous chapters too many to mention, and so I have picked out just a few – for amusement only and not to say that these are the top names.

Please take note that as we step back in time we must now refer to these productions as Pantomimes and not Pantos, as in the more modern vernacular.

## CHARLES PERRAULT

*1628–1703*
*Often referred to as 'The Grandfather of Pantomimes'*

The world of Pantomimes owes much to the seventeenth-century writer Charles Perrault, who was the author of eight fairy stories, six of which incredibly became the Pantomimes we know and love today. Just like the Brothers Grimm, he did not actually create the stories but committed to paper tales taken from folklore.

- The French author Charles Perrault was born in Paris on 12 January 1628, the son of Pierre Perrault and Paquette Le Clerc
- He benefited from a wealthy background and so he had the advantage of an excellent education at the best of schools, where he was always the top of his class
- He was a man who was interested in everything around him; he was progressive in his thoughts and preferred to move forward, favouring the modern and the future over the ancient and the past
- He studied law and then, after practising as a lawyer for some time, in 1664 he was appointed Chief Clerk in the King's Building Superintendent's Office
- In 1671 Charles Perrault became a member of the famous Académie Française
- In 1672 he married Marie Guichon with whom he went on to have five children
- It was Charles Perrault who is credited with saving the Tuileries Gardens for the people of Paris, when it was proposed to reserve them for royal use
- He is also famous for the stormy literary quarrel which unfavourably compared the ancient authors with modern writers and known universally as the *Quarrel of the Ancients and Moderns*
- He is best remembered for *Tales and Stories of the Past with Morals, with the subtitle: Tales of Mother Goose*
- Charles Perrault died in Paris on 16 May 1703

## AND FINALLY

- Charles Perrault was almost 70 years old when he actually wrote his first fairy tale in 1697
- Perrault used images from around him as the settings for his tales. For example, he used the Chateau Ussé as the backdrop for *Sleeping Beauty*

- His most famous tales are still in print to this day and have been made into stage plays, films, operas and, of course, into animated motion pictures by, for example, Walt Disney, as well as others
- Charles' brother, Claude, is remembered as the architect of the severe east range of the Louvre in Paris, which was built between 1665 and 1680 – now how proud must their parents have been to have two such talented children! So, if you are a supporter of the nature and not nurture theory, then quote these two gentlemen – along with the Brothers Grimm of course

## SOME OF PERRAULT'S WELL-KNOWN STORIES INCLUDE

*Bluebeard (Barbe Bleue)*
*Cinderella (Cendrillon)*
*Hop O' My Thumb (Le Petit Poucet)*
*Little Red Riding Hood (Le Petit Chaperon Rouge)*
*Puss in Boots (Le Chat Botté)*
*Ricky of the Tuft (Ricquet à la Houppe)*
*Sleeping Beauty (La Belle au Bois Dormant)*
*The Fairies (Les Fées)*

## JOHN RICH

*1681–1761*
*Often referred to as 'The Father of Pantomimes'*

John Rich was the son of English theatre manager Christopher Rich, and upon the death of his father inherited Lincoln's Inn Fields Theatre and is credited with introducing the true birth of Pantomime to the English theatre-goer. He wanted to be an actor himself but lacked the finer points of education which would have enabled a more intelligent delivery of lines and so, adopting the stage name of Lun, he turned his desire to perform to the silent role of Harlequin and was soon acclaimed as the finest performer of that part.

## THE RISE OF JOHN RICH

- Upon inheriting the Lincoln's Inn Fields Theatre John Rich set about restoring it before going into competition with Drury Lane Theatre by staging similar productions; the Pantomime war had begun
- He went on to present a unique form of two-part entertainments at his theatre with classical performances staged alongside comic episodes featuring characters from *commedia dell'arte*
- In 1717 the great John Weaver joined John Rich and it was from Weaver that Rich took the name Pantomime to describe his innovative, two-part productions. Weaver had originally used the word Pantomime to describe his own Ballets-Pantomimes that he believed were an accurate imitation of the Pantomimes originally performed in Ancient Rome. And so in this year the first production Rich billed as a Pantomime appeared on stage as *Harlequin Sorcerer*
- In 1721 Rich introduced to his Pantomime productions something that has now become an integral part of modern Pantomimes and that is topical references as a part of the script
- His Pantomimes grew in popularity and in the competition between Lincoln's Inn and Drury Lane to be the best, Lincoln's Inn stormed ahead
- John Rich was very proactive in the production of his Pantomimes; he not only wrote the comic scenes but also created the illusions and involved himself in the creation of the scenery. He was also interested in the theatrical practices of the day and was responsible for putting a stop to the ridiculous tradition of allowing privileged members of the public to wander wherever they wanted backstage and even onto the stage during a performance if they so desired! So, in many ways it is thanks to him that theatre is the enjoyable experience it is today

# JOSEPH GRIMALDI

*1778–1837*
*Clown of all clowns; the father of clowning, he was responsible for introducing the Dame into Pantomimes and reputedly for encouraging audience participation too*

- Joseph Grimaldi was born in Holborn, London on 18 December 1778. He was the illegitimate son of an Italian immigrant, Giuseppe Grimaldi, and Rebecca Brooker; he lived for most of his life in Clerkenwell
- He came from a theatrical family; his great-grandfather, Jean Baptist Grimaldi, was a comedian and a dancer – he was also a dentist who entertained his patients. Joseph's grandfather – Jean Baptist's son – was a fairground acrobat who was famous in mid-eighteenth-century Paris, France. It was in turn his son, Giuseppe, who settled in England around the year 1758 and who by this move ensured that we as a country could lay claim to the most famous clown of all times, Joseph Grimaldi!
- Joseph Grimaldi's father, Giuseppe, was Ballet Master at Drury Lane and his mother, Rebecca Brooker, was a dancer. So it was that the world of entertainment was a part of Joseph's life from the day he was born
- By the age of 2 years old Joseph Grimaldi was appearing on stage at Sadler's Wells with his father
- When Joseph was just 3 years old, he narrowly escaped an early death when impersonating a monkey on stage at Sadler's Wells. His father was swinging him on a chain when it unexpectedly and without warning broke; fortunately for Joe he was caught by a spectator
- He subsequently and frequently appeared as fairies and dwarfs at both Sadler's Wells and Drury Lane as well as in numerous other minor roles throughout his childhood, where he learned the craft and artistry upon which he came to rely. He then continued to work at both theatres for a period of forty-five years, both as a performer and later as a part proprietor at Sadler's Wells
- By 1789 the young Joseph Grimaldi was already playing to critical acclaim and enjoyed his first hit at the age of 16 years old when he played the hag Morag in *The Talisman of Orosmanes*, or *Harlequin Made Happy*, at Sadler's Wells
- He may have been a professional clown but his life was tinged with sadness – they do say that clowns frequently wear the mask of comedy to hide an inner sadness. His father died when he was 9 years old; his first wife, Maria, died in childbirth, along with their child and his son, from his second marriage to Mary Bristow, died of alcoholism before he was even 30 years old. So sadness played a huge part in this clown's life
- In 1806 Joseph Grimaldi made his debut at Covent Garden in *Harlequin and Mother Goose*, or *The Golden Egg*, a piece in which there was no

dialogue but just music; this was the start of his iconic career and a defining professional moment

- In 1812 Grimaldi played the part of Queen Ronabellyana in *Harlequin and the Red Dwarf*, and later he played the Baroness in *Harlequin and Cinderella*. This has since been hailed as the birth of the Pantomime Dame

- It was Joseph Grimaldi who invented clown make-up with that eerie, almost sinister grin, so designed that it would be visible from the back of Drury Lane auditorium and the distinctive white face with two red half-moons painted on his cheeks, which later became a permanent trademark of the clown

- In 1823, at the age of just 45 years, ill health and exhaustion forced Grimaldi into early retirement and by 1828 he was penniless

- His financial situation was eased by monies raised at benefit performances and a pension granted to him from the Drury Lane Theatrical Fund

- He spent the last years of his life at the the Marquis of Cornwallis pub in Pentonville, where it is said that the landlord carried him home on his back at the end of each day

- Joseph Grimaldi died aged 59 on 21 May 1837

## AND FINALLY

- Grimaldi was a skilled dancer, mime artist and acrobat as well as an actor
- The name Joey – taken from *Joseph* Grimaldi – is now a part of the English language and has come to be the word we use for a 'clown'
- It is unsurprising that exhaustion eventually caught up with Joseph Grimaldi and became his downfall, for at one point he was for several years appearing at two theatres on a nightly basis, running from one to the other
- He created clowns that combined the rogue with the simpleton and the criminal with the innocent all in the one character; his white face became his trademark and was later adopted by all clowns
- One of Grimaldi's best known and loved songs was 'Hot Codlins':

*A little old woman, her living she got by selling*
*Hot codlins, hot, hot, hot.*

*And this little old woman, who codlins sold, tho' her codlins were hot,*
*She felt herself cold.*
*So to keep herself warm she thought it no sin*
*To fetch for herself a quartern of …*

Grimaldi would then pause and the audience would excitedly shout out yell, 'Gin!' at which point he would look at them with a sort of reprimanding disgust and reply, '*Oh! For shame*'

## THE LITTLERS

The world of entertainment has always been renowned for its theatrical dynasties; we refer to a family as being a theatrical dynasty when almost the entire family is dedicated to and immersed in the world of entertainment – families such as the Redgraves and the Mills fall into this category. It comes as no surprise then to know that Pantomime has some of its own dynasties and one of these is the Littler family, comprising brothers Sir Emile Littler and Prince Littler CBE and their sister, Blanche Littler, who were at one time three of the most powerful people in the world of theatre and were descended from parents who were also in the world of theatre.

They began their careers producing shows of both straight drama and musicals – and by the mid-1930s were producing Pantomimes in the West End. Emile even married the renowned Principal Boy actress Cora Griffin, thereby expanding the dynasty. This union was followed by Prince also marrying within the business, and as with Emile, he too married a Pantomime star by the name of Nora Delaney – and so their Empire grew even bigger.

The Littler trio ruled the West End with their Pantomimes for the next twenty years and soon it became apparent that whilst Emile and Blanche were happier on the artistic side of theatre, writing and producing Pantomimes, Prince's expertise was leaning more and more towards the business side of what was fast becoming the Littler Empire – although that is not to say that he didn't produce, for he did, and quite prolifically too.

## AND FINALLY

- During the 1950s Emile and Prince Littler wrote and produced more than 15 Pantomimes which played in the West End of London and a further 200 Pantomimes which played in the Provinces
- A Littler Pantomime could boast a chorus of over fifty, something unheard of today when budgets rarely stretch to more than a dozen – excluding the Babes, of course
- The Littlers were well known for their charity work
- They also produced many successful West End musicals
- Emile Littler was knighted in 1974
- Prince Littler was awarded the CBE

*Chapter 6*

# PANTOMIME PRODUCERS

*The Men and Women at the Helm of the Production Liners*

## THE PANTO PRODUCER

I suppose we must first answer the question: what is a Producer? Well, the way I always answer that question is probably in the simplest of ways by saying a producer is a production's parent; he/she is the father/mother of the entire show. It is the producer who gives birth to the production, feeding and nurturing it until it reaches the maturity of first night. A producer makes sure that the right team is in place all along the way, just as a parent would make sure that the right teachers and friends surround their much-loved child. As a parent would provide a secure and loving home in which a child could thrive, then so too does the producer provide the right venue for his baby to grow and thrive. Like any good parent, the producer injects money into their baby to ensure a good end result and then like any good parent they understand that even when up and running the care must go on.

Continuing on the analogous theme, staging a production is a bit like making a journey in a car. Most cars will get you from A to B, but it is the driver who will make the journey successful, comfortable and safe. It is the driver upon whom the passengers ultimately depend, for if he drives erratically or dangerously then it affects everyone on board; alternatively the driver can make the journey both pleasurable and successful with the final destination reached on time, a destination that can in many cases be the provider of fun and enjoyment. It is pretty much the same in the world of theatre, for staging a production is a journey of its own kind and in order to put on any type of successful theatrical production there must be in place a first class producer to drive the operation forward and take the cast and crew to the final and successful destination of opening night and Panto is no exception to this rule. It is totally irrelevant whether the production in question is amateur or professional, the rules remains the same, for once a good producer is at the helm of a production then the chances of success, if not guaranteed, are certainly stronger than those of a production company with a weak and ineffectual producer at the helm.

On the amateur scene, there are many, many amateur Pantos produced each year throughout the UK in draughty village halls through to the large and splendid halls of our grand, public schools; there are equally many, many professional Pantos produced too, ranging from, in their case, the small scale touring companies who visit community centres and educational establishments, through to the star-studded productions playing at 2,000+ seat theatres. However, whatever the situation or status – amateur or professional – all Pantos have one thing in common and that is that each and every one of them must, or at the very least should, have at the helm a producer of the highest calibre and certainly one suited to the situation in hand. As an example, the priorities of a village-hall Panto producer will be vastly different to those of the producer of a large-scale commercial Panto. As a prime example, the village-hall production is generally more about community spirit and local involvement than in making a monetary profit, which of course is what the commercial Panto is rightly all about; each though being the correct, appropriate approach in the circumstances and each having its own rightful place in the thespian world.

In the professional theatre there are true and real master producers of Pantos, just as there are true and real masters of any profession. At first glance it may seem like a rather attractive job – only working over the Christmas period! – but sadly for those involved in the production of Panto this is, of course, not the case, for as we all know success is in the art of pedantic preparation and so, for the Panto producer, as one season ends then so then another one begins.

In the professional world there are many companies for whom Panto production is only a part of their extensive production programme, but whom never-the-less focus wholeheartedly on producing Pantos of the highest calibre, one such company being Qdos. In fact, the very name Qdos is synonymous with Panto, for they are now recognised as the ultimate experts in Panto production. So with this in mind it made perfect sense for me to talk to them, a task I approached with some trepidation. Quite often when a writer, albeit in the name of research, approaches a company and actually has the audacity to ask for an interview with either 'the man at the top' or at the very least someone of significant importance, it is at that very moment that a brick wall appears. But not so when I approached Qdos, for here it quickly became apparent that as a company they were as welcoming, happy, helpful and jolly as any one of their productions; could this then be the secret of their success? So who are they?

# QDOS ENTERTAINMENT LTD

## CAPTAIN OF THE SHIP

I have always been a great believer in a ship is only as good as its captain and have seen many companies flounder when 'the man at the top' changes. Therefore, I was intrigued to discover more about whoever was at the helm of this enormous vessel, and so it was that I discovered the captain of this particular ship to be a certain Nick Thomas, Chairman of Qdos Entertainment Ltd.

## NICK THOMAS, THE MAN AND HIS LIFE

- Nick Thomas was born on 16 December 1959 in Blandford Forum, Dorset
- He is the youngest of five children
- In 1968 he moved with his family to Scarborough in North Yorkshire
- A talented puppeteer, he won the television contest *New Faces* in 1975
- In 1982 he started his career in production back in Scarborough – also noted for being the adopted home of that great British playwright Alan Aykbourn – with the *Keith Harris Show*
- It was also in 1982 that Nick Thomas started his theatre production business and in the same year met his future wife, Sandra, with whom he went on to have two daughters

- By 1992 he was producing several summer seasons and Pantos each year
- 1998 saw Nick Thomas recognised as the world's no. 1 producer of Pantos as well as being a major leading talent manager
- In 1999 the company Qdos Entertainment was born
- Further along the line, he then acquired various smaller companies enabling his to grow into the company it is today
- In 2008 Nick Thomas was publicly recognised by the *Stage* newspaper as one of the 'Top 10 Most Influential Figures of the Decade' in entertainment

## BY HIS SIDE – MICHAEL HARRISON

Great men, however, rarely stand alone and in fact the strength and powers of their leadership qualities can be often be judged by the team with which they surround themselves. This is true of all business and government ventures from the President of America to the chairman of a production company. Nick Thomas must be acutely aware of this for he surrounded himself with a first-class team and none more so than – at the time of going to press – Mr Michael Harrison, Managing Director, Qdos Entertainment's Pantomime Division.

To date Michael Harrison has produced over fifty Pantos for Nick Thomas and therefore for Qdos; he has also written and directed numerous others. It is he who is responsible for the now-legendary, record-breaking Newcastle Theatre Royal Pantos, in addition to directing productions at Plymouth Theatre Royal and at the Birmingham Hippodrome. But he too is not just a 'Panto person' and has produced many other productions, including *Chess*, which was directed by Craig Revel Horwood, *Aspects of Love*, starring David Essex, *The Witches of Eastwick*, starring Marti Pellow, *Jolson & Co.*, starring Allan Stewart, and *The Bodyguard* at London's Adelphi Theatre.

## THE COMPANY THAT IS THE QDOS ENTERTAINMENT GROUP

- The Qdos Entertainment Group itself employs over 800 full-time staff across its 4 divisions
- Although the Panto division has only 18 full-time members of staff, it takes a further 1,000 seasonal workers to put a Panto together; these include: actors/actresses, musicians, dancer/singers, creative teams, stage staff, technical and production staff
- It is the only production company to stage Pantos in England, Scotland, Wales *and* Northern Ireland
- The number of Panto productions mounted by Qdos is continually growing and worldwide in excess of 1.2 million people watch a Qdos Panto each Christmas, with this number increasing on an annual basis
- *Cinderella* is currently the most popular of all the Pantos Qdos stage
- Each Panto production is led by an executive producer. This executive producer is then responsible for writing each script, casting and engaging the services of freelance directors, choreographers and lighting designers
- Although Qdos is 'famous for' its spectacular Panto productions, it is oh so much more and is currently the UK's second largest privately owned regional theatre operator with its portfolio including Cliffs Pavilion (Southend), Palace Theatre (Westcliff), Swan Theatre (HighWycombe), Wyvern Theatre (Swindon), Beck Theatre (Hayes) White Rock Theatre (Hastings) Orchard Theatre (Dartford) Watford Colosseum, G Live (Guildford) and Crewe Lyceum Theatre
- In addition to Panto productions Qdos has also produced shows for national tours and for the West End, including *Boogie Nights – The 70s Musical, Boogie Nights 2 – Happy Days the Musical, The King and I*, London Palladium, *This is Elvis, Elaine Paige in Concert, Joe Pasquale Live, The Chuckle Brothers Live* and *Simply Ballroom*, London, Las Vegas and worldwide touring
- As a part of its comprehensive production programme, Qdos also produces lavish 'own-brand' production shows for the American based Celebrity Cruise Line. As a company it is also the largest provider of leisure-sector entertainment and related services in the UK through its subsidiary The Entertainment Department (UK) Ltd – TED. The company delivers a 'turn-key' service from concept through development

to delivery of staff, performers, production shows, training programmes, audio visual provision. TED clients include Thomson Holidays, Park Resorts and Parkdean Holidays, First Choice and G Casinos

- A part of the Qdos company includes the Talent Division, Qtalent Ltd, which is the new name for the combined agencies International Artistes and JLM Personal Management. These two agencies between them have 100 years of expertise and know-how in the British entertainment industry. This combined talent-management resource now forms a unique and powerful force in the field of film, television and theatre in the UK and beyond. The company has a prestigious and diverse roster of high-profile performers and actors, as well as many of the UK's top writers, producers and directors, including Ronnie Corbett, Shane Richie and the Chuckle Brothers. Qvoice Ltd is one of the leading British voice agencies and represents well-known voices for commercials, film and television, including Ricky Gervais, Bill Nighy and Dannii Minogue

## SOME FASCINATING QDOS PANTO FACTS

- The Qdos Panto season takes £25 million at the box office each year and is still growing
- Qdos keeps its sets and props in a huge 80,000sq ft warehouse, which is actually bigger than most supermarkets!
- Qdos has over 50 Panto sets, 3,500 scenic backdrops and a staggering 150,000 costumes
- Each November it takes more than 100 articulated lorries to deliver the sets and costumes to the 24 theatres around the country
- Qdos has the country's biggest and most impressive Panto archive which houses old programmes, posters, leaflets, Panto memorabilia, as well as a few of Danny La Rue's magnificent Panto costumes
- Qdos' Pantos are headlined by actors and entertainers from the world of stage, television and film for it would seem that 'names' are crowd pullers, encouraging those who might not otherwise go along to see a Panto but would go to see their favourite star perform in the flesh; such stars as John Barrowman, Joe Pasquale, Brian Conley, Julian Clary, Nigel Havers, Lynda Bellingham, Gok Wan, Craig Revel Horwood, Christopher Biggins and Elaine C. Smith to name but just a few. In the past, Qdos has worked with many of the Panto greats, including Danny La Rue, John Inman, Ronnie Corbett, Paul O'Grady, Rolf Harris and Frankie Howerd

- In 2011 Qdos recognising the popularity of Anne Widdecombe, immediately signed her for the Panto *Snow White and the Seven Dwarfs* in which she played for two seasons

## AND FINALLY

- Over the years Nick Thomas has built Qdos Entertainment Ltd into one of the largest groups in Europe, specialising not only in the production of Pantos but also in other productions, as well as specialising in venue management, contract catering and talent management
- He has homes both in Central London and in North Yorkshire – as a Yorkshire lass myself, born and bred, I naturally attribute his expertise and success to his connections with Yorkshire; we're a grand lot, aye by gum, we are!

And so we conclude our look at Qdos with the thought that although they may be a *large* Panto producing company they are by no means the *only* producing company on the Panto circuit. There are other excellent companies out there too and deciding just which and how many companies to feature was actually very tricky. In the end it was only lack of space that prohibited me featuring all those I really wanted to include. For that reason and that reason alone I went for the most prominent of the other companies, though of course some may disagree with my choice – and that's okay, because we are, after all, working in a business of personal opinions, that may or may not be right. And so we move on to the second producer to be featured here, and that is …

## FIRST FAMILY ENTERTAINMENT

Kevin Wood was working as a successful independent producer of Pantomimes when, in 1995, he set up First Family Entertainment (FFE) as a division of the Ambassadors Theatre Group, with the sole purpose of producing Pantos, Pantos that would then be housed in ATG theatres. This shrewd business move ensured that the profits would stay within the same company and not be distributed between the receiving house and the producing company. This in turn meant that the income generated could, of course, be reinvested in the productions themselves; this is a unique approach to the production of Pantomime.

## KEVIN WOOD – THE MAN AND HIS LIFE

- Kevin Wood was born in 1951 in Deale, Kent
- He has two younger brothers, and it would seem a family where entertainment is in the blood, for Kevin's grandparents were in the entertainment business before him and his younger brother Anthony (Tony Wood) is the renowned BAFTA-winning British TV producer
- Kevin was educated at Dover Grammar School before going to Nottingham University in 1970, where he studied social sciences
- In 1973 Kevin graduated from Nottingham with a 2:1 degree in social science, after which he went into retail management, joining the Graduate Management Training Scheme at Marks & Spencer. However, his artistic side refused to be repressed and he resigned just seven months later
- In 1974, his theatrical aspirations now released, Kevin took up a position as ASM at the Library Theatre, Scarborough, North Yorkshire – the home of that other great thespian Alan Aykbourn. Remember too that Nick Thomas, in the previous piece, was also associated with Scarborough? What is it with this little seaside town in the North East of the UK that attracts those with artistic leanings! And so once again I am proud to be Yorkshire
- In 1976 Kevin Wood married Helga Wood, a set and costume designer; not only did they keep the profession in the family, but the name too!
- Together Kevin and Helga went on to have two daughters and a son, with all three children destined not only for theatrical careers, but it transpired as Panto specialists too
- In 2005, after twenty-five years as an independent producer, Kevin created FFE, with offices in Covent Garden – the heart of theatre land – and these offices remain to this day in Covent Garden, with him as Chief Executive and Producer
- In 2012 he married choreographer Sarah Dean

## AND FINALLY

- Kevin has achieved all he initially set out to achieve but he still has so many more goals and projects up his sleeve. It is like they say: 'Tread the boards just once and you walk amongst the stars forever.' No retirement for you then, Kevin Wood!

## SOME INTERESTING FACTS ABOUT FIRST FAMILY ENTERTAINMENT

- The first year FFE produced Pantos, they produced eight; this year they will produce ten. It is unlikely, however, that they will produce more than twelve a year in the future, preferring to concentrate on the quality of their productions rather than the quantity
- FFE has approximately 15 full-time employees all year round, but during the Christmas period that figure rises to a staggering 600 seasonal employees
- Making sure that the sets and costumes are performance worthy are the staff at the Nottingham based workshops and storage units. Here is where the sets and props are made and where existing costumes are maintained and new ones created
- Each year twenty-four lorries leave the FFE base in Nottingham to carry and distribute the sets, props and costumes to the various theatres throughout the UK
- FFE's policy is to present well-known entertainers to the Panto audiences; entertainers such as Barbara Windsor, Ashleigh and Pudsey, Justin Fletcher, Paul O'Grady, Ruby Wax, Louie Spence, Cilla Black, Darius Campbell, Russell Grant, Jennifer Ellison, Tina O'Brien, John Barrowman, Simon Callow, Stephen Gately, Susan Hampshire, Nigel Havers, Ross Kemp, Patsy Kensit, Kim and Aggie, Kym Marsh, Richard O'Brien, Suzanne Shaw, Simon Shepherd, Elaine C. Smith, Twiggy, Toyah Willcox, Richard Wilson, Joanna Page, Gareth Gates, Alistair McGowan and Jonathan Wilkes
- This company was the first production company to entice artists from across the Atlantic to appear in this great British tradition, and so it was that artists such as Priscilla Presley, Pamela Anderson, Henry Winkler, Patrick Duffy, Mickey Rooney, Jan Rooney, Steve Guttenberg, Paul Michael Glaser, Dirk Benedict and David Hasselhoff made their pantomime debuts for FFE

And now on we go to look at UK Productions …

# UK PRODUCTIONS

## THE CAPTAIN OF THE UK PRODUCTIONS SHIP

At the helm of this theatre-going liner is a certain Martin Dodd and it is Martin who, as the company's director, ensures that UK Productions, which is dedicated to the production of both Panto and musicals, maintains its position as one of the leading producers in these fields, both nationally and internationally.

## MARTIN DODD – THE MAN AND HIS LIFE

- Martin Dodd was born on the 29 January 1963 in the village of New Longton, near Preston, Lancashire, the youngest son of Alan and Margery Dodd
- His older brother, Peter, is the Sales and Marketing Director for *Welcome to Yorkshire*
- Martin was educated at Hutton Grammar School in Hutton, near Preston, Lancashire
- Whilst at school, he dreamt of a career in the entertainment industry and so at the tender age of 11 years old he joined a touring concert party, initially as a solo piano accordionist but then he developed his act to include stand-up comedy and tap dancing! A clear case of focus and determination, something I tell my students is necessary to be successful in the entertainment business
- After finishing his A levels and leaving school and, more importantly, whilst his friends were taking their gap years in exotic far off lands, Martin auditioned for Pontins Holidays. He wanted to be a Blue Coat entertainer and follow in the footsteps of many top variety artists that have honed their craft in this very special environment – focus and determination strike again!
- In 1981 Martin went to London University where he studied religion and sociology, for which he was awarded a BA (Hons) degree. Whilst

there he also spent two summer seasons in Weymouth and two summer and Christmas seasons in Paignton, so satisfying both his intellectual and entertainment needs at the same time

- After this, he completed his MSc in recreation management at Loughborough University
- He wanted to be an entertainer and he wanted to fly – not like the birds, of course, Martin wanted to fly airplanes! And so, whilst at university, he was accepted as a pilot with the Royal Air Force Volunteer Reserve on a university air squadron for three very happy years and guess what? He became the Squadron Entertainment Officer – focus and determination once more to the fore!
- Martin left university in debt – as do all students – and so had to take on a 'normal' job to pay off these debts
- His first job was with the London Borough of Bexley where he was responsible for developing a broad entertainment programme across a number of venues both indoors and outdoors. Needless to say, having crossed the line he never went back to performing, but no matter he was still in the entertainment industry, just a different branch that's all
- In 1987 Martin Wood took over the 1,500-seat Civic Theatre in Guildford, which is where his love of Panto production really began to take a hold, for it was during his first year there that he brought Panto to the Civic Theatre
- In 1990 he moved to Portsmouth to manage the 2,228-seat Guildhall and associated outdoor events programme
- It wasn't possible to produce Panto at this venue but in the search for an alternative in the form of a musical, UK Productions was born; the year was 1995
- The first musical for UK Productions, *Barnum*, was originally planned as a two-theatre production between Guildford and Portsmouth, but in fact turned into an eighteen-month national tour
- Many more musicals and Pantos followed. Martin also took the Guildhall and events management from the public to the private sector during this period and continued to oversee the management for a further twelve years
- He has also worked on a number of unique events including the nation's fiftieth anniversary of D-Day commemorations for Her Majesty's Government. Amongst other things, he produced a state banquet, with

700 guests, for 14 visiting heads of state, including Her Majesty the Queen and President Bill Clinton, the Tour de France in the south of England and Portsmouth's 800th anniversary and VE Day celebrations. Martin's focus and determination have certainly brought him a long way from that naïve, 11-year old piano accordionist with a penchant for stand-up comedy and tap dancing

## UK PRODUCTIONS AND THEIR PANTOMIMES

UK Productions put into their Panto mix the very best of star names from television, film and stage, plus a wealth of talented performers, together with lavish sets and costumes, all in order to produce each year a fresh and new product about which they are passionate – Pantomime.

Because UK Productions produce both commercial musical theatre and Pantos their creative teams, who work on both are, as a result, able to bring a greater diversity to the two. As a company they are meticulous about the care of their sets and costumes which, as one Panto season ends, are refurbished and cleaned, with new ones produced each year ready for the start of the next season. This is in addition to the all-important scripts which, of course, need to be reviewed and updated each year as Panto is, by tradition, a very topical art form in terms of its music, comedy and dialogue content. This is a process that, by its very nature, must go on not only up until opening night but throughout the entire Panto run too. For if one day something newsworthy happens, then a seasoned Panto-goer would quite rightly expect a reference to it somewhere in the dialogue by the first performance of that day.

## SOME FASCINATING UK PRODUCTION COMPANY FACTS

- Head office for UK Productions is in Godalming, Surrey
- The Scenery Store and Workshop is housed in Wem, Shropshire with the Costume Store and Workshop housed in Blackpool
- Their production department rents out Panto and musical sets as well as costumes nationally and internationally, and this is in addition to producing new sets, props and costumes for other producers
- Key staff at UK Productions are Production Manager Andy Batty, who has been with the company since its inception and who oversees the

production design, installation and running for all of the Pantos and musicals, and Head of Wardrobe Elizabeth Dennis, who is also the company's costume designer for its Pantos and musicals

- UK Productions have also produced shows internationally in Malaysia, Turkey, Greece, Malta, Ireland, New Zealand and Italy, as well as in London's West End
- The 2013/14 season sees twenty-five productions going out over the Christmas period, including eleven of their own Pantos. It is an ever growing company with a focused and determined Martin Dodd at the helm

## AND FINALLY

- In addition to Pantos, the musicals produced by UK productions include *7 Brides for 7 Brothers, Oklahoma!, Singin' in the Rain*, Disney's *Beauty & the Beast, South Pacific, Jekyll and Hyde – The Musical, Carousel, Fiddler on the Roof, Anything Goes, The Pirates of Penzance, 42nd Street* and *Barnum*
- Working closely with Wayne Sleep OBE, UK Productions have also produced three original dance shows, *World of Classical Ballet, Aspects of Dance* and *Ready Steady Dance*
- UK Productions have produced a number of outdoor events too and were responsible for the creation and production of *The Stansted Park Proms*, an annual 2-day, open-air concert playing to up to 10,000 people a night in the grounds of Stansted House, a stately home in the heart of Hampshire

To close this chapter we will now look at the man who is affectionately known throughout the entertainment industry as 'The King of Panto' and that man is Paul Elliott. I always, before I start to write a piece on anyone at all, ask around the industry and talk to people who know the person concerned; that way before I become immersed in factual research I have a real feel for the person. In the case of Paul Elliott, I was always met with comments such as, 'Oh a lovely man' … 'A real gentleman' … 'One of the best in the industry'. I was intrigued, as I had never actually personally met him. I almost felt obliged to like him and that it would be a treasonable offence not to do so!

# PAUL ELLIOTT

*Actor, Director, Producer and Playwright AND 'The King of Pantomime'*

- Paul Elliott was born on 9 December 1941 in Bournemouth, the only child of Lewis and Sybil Elliott, who owned a fruit and vegetable shop
- He was educated Bournemouth School
- After leaving school he worked selling fridges in a Bournemouth department store
- Paul had no formal training as an actor, but enjoyed acting at school and performed in various amateur groups. It was at one of these performances that he was 'spotted' by the producer of the Barry O'Brien Company, who had a season at the Palace Court Theatre. As a result, he was invited to join the group. 'Why not?' thought the young Paul Elliott
- And so it was that in 1958 Paul Elliott made his first professional appearance on stage at the Palace Court Theatre in Bournemouth, for which he was paid the princely sum of £5 a week
- In the 1960s Paul appeared in the renowned and much-loved BBC TV series *Dixon of Dock Green* where he played Cadet Michael Bonnet. He was a member of the cast for two years and it was on this programme that he met and forged a relationship with Peter Byrne, who was later to become his business partner and the other half of the production company E. & B. Productions – Elliott and Byrne
- In 1963 Paul decided that he wanted to produce theatre, and so in the same year he joined forces with Michael Gaunt and formed Gaul Productions, presenting his first professional production at the Rhyl Little Theatre in North Wales
- In 1964 he formed the above mentioned E. & B. Productions and subsequently toured a production of *Ring For Catty*. It was Paul Elliott and Peter Byrne's first venture together – and it lost money! Thankfully, they didn't give up though and went on to enjoy great and then even greater success

- In 1967 Paul began a working relationship with Duncan C. Weldon, another renowned theatrical producer, and they went on to produce together for ten years, as Triumph Entertainment Ltd, later returning to work together yet again in 2001. Together they have produced, or co-produced, 300 London productions, with *When We Are Married* being the first in 1969
- It was in 1968 that Paul Elliott produced his first Panto at The New Theatre, Hull. The Panto was *Goldilocks and the Three Bears*
- In 1987 Paul Elliott married Linda Hayden, an actress, and together they went on to have two children, Hadyn and Laura Jane. Laura Jane grew up to be account manager at AKA, the foremost London theatrical advertising agency, and Haydn went on to study at Oxford Brooks University
- After the momentous decision to become a producer, Paul went on to stage productions on a worldwide basis. He produced Panto for seven years in Canada, these mainly starring Lionel Blair
- In 1997 Paul's production of *Jolson* won an Olivier Award for Best Musical
- In 1999 he sold his Pantomime business to Nick Thomas of Qdos, after which he worked with Qdos as consultant and executive producer/director and writer until 2013
- In 1999 another of Paul's productions, *Kat and the Kings* won an Olivier Award for Best Musical
- In 2001 more awards came to Paul Elliott Productions – an Olivier and an *Evening Standard* Award for *Stones in His Pockets*
- In 2002, together with Duncan C. Weldon, Paul won the prestigious Tony Award on Broadway for *Private Lives* with Alan Rickman and Lindsey Duncan
- In 2006 Paul's first work as a playwright hit the stage; entitled *There's No Place Like Home*, to date it has toured nationally on three separate occasions
- During his career Paul has produced around a staggering 450 Pantos and after 45 years producing, directing and writing he finally retired from Panto Land after the 2012/13 season had completed
- The King also produced, directed and wrote for eleven consecutive years at the Kings Theatre, Edinburgh

- At the height of his Panto career he produced no less than twenty-nine shows in one Christmas season alone – which begs the question from where does this extraordinary man get his energy?
- In 1999 Paul formed Paul Elliott Ltd, and in 2000 he returned to work with Duncan C. Weldon – Triumph Entertainment Ltd – on other plays and musicals
- In 2012 Paul Elliott was awarded a Fellowship of the Arts from the University of Bournemouth in recognition for his work as a theatrical producer

## AND FINALLY

- Paul Elliott describes one of the lesser known Pantos, *Goldilocks*, as his 'Lucky Mascot Pantomime', the reason being that it was the first ever Panto he produced in Hull all those years ago, and so when he was invited to expand to other theatres he always chose *Goldilocks* as the first production. His mascot has certainly worked for him
- Paul's autobiography is entitled *Keeping My Balls in the Air* and is (quote) 'a rambling story of a Theatrical Producer!'
- In addition to *There's No Place Like Home*, Paul also co-wrote *Hot Flush* (four British tours) and *Rave on, Jolson – The Fact and the Fiction* and *The Good, the Bad and the Funny*
- And the final word goes to the King himself who, after years of hard work, insists he doesn't need a holiday but instead says 'To me this *IS* a holiday'

And the final, 'final' word is from me. Paul Elliott is everything I was told he would be – and more! This man is true entertainment royalty and he really does deserve to wear the crown and be hailed as 'the King of Panto'.

*Chapter 7*

# WHO? WHAT? WHERE? WHEN?

## ANSWERS TO SOME OF THOSE IRRITATING LITTLE QUESTIONS

A little knowledge is a dangerous thing, or so they say anyway. Well, I suppose that might be the case if you attempt brain surgery knowing only that the brain is situated somewhere above the shoulders! However, in the general, run of the mill situations then a little knowledge can make you feel at least a little less stupid than you would otherwise feel. But, you know what, at best that little bit of knowledge could perhaps sow a seed of interest which might just in fact one day develop into a lifelong passion.

In this section are answers to some questions that might have just been bugging you for some length of time and if that is not the case, then you might wonder why they weren't bugging you! I will start by introducing some more of the famous names in the world of Panto, so you will have a better idea of who's who after reading this section.

## WHO?

### ANDREINI, FRANCESCO

He was an Italian actor-manager, as well as a playwright; he was also the senior member of a celebrated family of *commedia dell'arte* players.

### ASKEY, ARTHUR

Arthur Askey (1900–82) was a popular Panto performer who was known affectionately as 'Big-hearted Arthur' (or 'Big-hearted Martha' when he played the part of the Dame!). He was a tiny man with a big personality which endeared him to his audiences, with whom he had an easy and great rapport. He is remembered by the more 'mature' generation for his amusingly visual performance of 'The Bee Song', which is reproduced below as a reminder to all those who never tired of his performance of the song, be it in Panto or elsewhere for that matter. For those of you too young to remember – well, this is what you missed, good clean fun, sadly now long gone!

### The Bee Song

*Oh what a glorious thing to be*
*A healthy grown up busy, busy bee*
*Whiling away*
*The passing hours*
*Pinching all the pollen*
*From the cauliflow'rs*
*I'd like to be a busy little bee*
*Being just as busy as a bee can be*
*Flying round the garden*
*Brightest ever seen,*
*Taking back the honey*
*To the dear old queen.*

### Chorus

*Bz bz bz bz, honey bee, honey bee*
*Bz if you like but don't sting me*
*Bz bz bz bz, honey bee, honey bee*
*Bz if you like but don't sting me*

*Oh what a glorious thing to be*
*A healthy grown up busy, busy bee*
*Toying with the tulips*
*Tasting ev'ry type*
*Building up the honeycomb*
*That looks like tripe*
*I'd like to be a busy little bee*
*Being just as busy as a bee can be*
*Flying all around*
*In the wild hedgerows*

147

*Stinging all the cows*
*Upon the parson's nose*

*Chorus*

*Oh what a glorious thing to be,*
*A healthy grown up busy, busy bee,*
*Visiting the picnics,*
*Quite a little tease,*
*Raising little lumps*
*Upon the maidens' knees.*
*I'd like to be a busy little bee*
*Being just as busy as a bee can be,*
*Flirting with the butterfly*
*Strong upon the wing.*
*Whoopee! O death*
*Where is thy sting?*

*Chorus*

## BARD, WILKIE

Real name William Augustus Smith (1870–1944), Wilkie Bard was one of the most popular Dames to appear in Panto during the first half of the twentieth century. He became known for his bald wig and spotted eyebrows as well as for songs such as 'I Want to Sing in Opera' and 'Popping In and Out'. It was also thanks to him that tongue-twisters became an integral part of Panto, tongue-twisters such as 'The Leith Police Dismisseth Us' and 'She Sells Sea Shells on the Sea Shore'.

## BLANCHARD, EDWARD LEMAN

Edward Leman Blanchard (1820–89) was an English author whose Pantos dominated the Victorian theatre for almost forty years and who wrote in rhyming couplets. His scripts were used in many of the most spectacular productions at Drury Lane, London; in fact, Pantos written by Blanchard played at this theatre for 37 years and by the time of his death he had collaborated on more than 100 productions. In 1874 no less than four of his

Pantos were playing simultaneously at London theatres. Maybe he was the nineteenth-century equivalent of Andrew Lloyd Webber in terms of simultaneously running productions.

## BUCKSTONE, JOHN BALDWIN

Buckstone was an English Panto writer, actor and manager of the nineteenth century and wrote various highly successful Pantos for the Victorian stage.

## BYRON, H(ENRY) J(AMES)

Byron gave up his studies in medicine and law for the theatre and subsequently became a highly influential writer of Pantos. He also became known as the master of puns in his writing.

## CÉLESTE, CÉLINE

Céline Céleste (1814–42) was a French actress who some believe was the first of the modern Principal Boys in Panto. However, maybe this was wishful thinking on their part for it is in fact known that there were at least two other mature actresses who played Principal Boy before her.

## CHINESE POLICEMEN

The Chinese Policemen are a comedy double act – often in the plot of *Aladdin* – and are the pursuers of the Baddies going under bizarre names such as Ping and Pong or Bamboo and Typhoo. They are generally skilled in the art of slapstick and trick-work, which makes the chase routines more comedic.

## CHU-CHIN-CHOW

This is a musical comedy based on the Panto *Ali Baba and the Forty Thieves* and was very popular in the early twentieth century.

## CINQUEVALLI, PAUL – PAUL KESTNER

An English juggler born in Poland and a speciality act of the late Victorian Panto, Cinquevalli (1859–1918) only took up juggling after an accident prevented him from developing his career as a trapeze artist; he then became the most skilled juggler ever seen.

## COLLINS, LOTTIE

Lottie Collins (1866–1910) was an English singer and one of the leading Principal Girls of the late Victorian Panto and famous for the song 'Ta-Ra-Ra-Boom-De-Ay'. She first sang this song in *Dick Whittington* at the Grand Theatre in Islington, and it became her signature tune throughout her entire Panto career.

## DAINTY, BILLY

Billy Dainty (1927–86) was an English comedian who had a long, successful career in Panto, having made his first appearance at the tender age of just 12 years old. From this starting point he then worked his way up through such lowly roles as the back end of the cow and then upwards and onwards to the role of Dame, a role that he continued to play for thirty years.

## DE LOUTHERBOURG, PHILIPPE JACQUES

Trained in Paris, De Loutherbourg (1740–1812) was the acclaimed German artist, stage designer and scene painter for Pantos – and other productions – which were staged by David Garrick at Drury Lane in the late eighteenth century. He was a great innovator and introduced many new ideas to theatre.

## DELPINI, CARLO ANTONIO

Delpini (1740–1828) was an Italian actor credited with 'inventing' the Regency Panto.

## DUGGAN, MAGGIE

Maggie Duggan (1860–1919) was an English actress and one of the most popular Principal Boys of the late nineteenth century. She made her debut in Panto as a child and later her debut as Principal Boy in Liverpool.

## FYFFE, WILL

Will Fyffe (1885–1947) was a Scottish singer and comedian known for playing Dame in Panto and singing the song 'I Belong to Glasgae'.

## GARRICK, DAVID

An English actor and playwright, David Garrick (1717–79), as the manager of Drury Lane Theatre, was a major influence on the development of Panto.

## GREENWOOD, T(HOMAS) L(ONGDEN)

Greenwood (1806–79) was one of the most popular writers of Panto for the early Victorian stage.

## HARRIS, SIR AUGUSTUS HENRY GLOSSOP

Harris (1852–96) was an English theatre manager who was renowned for the spectacular Pantos at Drury Lane, Pantos that earned him the nickname 'The Father of Modern Panto'. He became the theatre's manager at the extraordinarily young age of 28. He is also remembered for taking the new and controversial step of casting stars of the music hall in his Pantos – rather similar to the casting of soap stars and pop stars today. He is also credited with making a Panto the sole piece of entertainment in an evening where before his time it had only been a part of an evening's entertainment. He did indeed change the face of Panto.

## HOWERD, FRANKIE

An English comedian and Panto star, Frankie Howerd (1921–92) was loved and admired for his apparently spontaneous asides to the audience and his conversations with the various animals found in Pantos.

## JOEY

This is the traditional name given to all clowns in honour of Joseph Grimaldi, who is acknowledged to have been the greatest clown ever to have walked the stage. Comic business in a Panto is sometimes referred to as Joey-Joey in his memory.

## LA RUE, DANNY

The famous female impersonator brought a touch of glamour to the role of Dame after the Second World War, as opposed to the ridiculous, as he played his Dames essentially female rather than as, in the time-honoured tradition, the masculine Dame.

## LACY, GEORGE

George Lacy (1904–89) made his stage debut at the age of 12 years and played the part of a Dame when he was only 24 years old. He is the performer who is credited with being the first Dame to specialise in outrageous and extravagant costumes. He wore a new outfit for virtually every scene, the most famous of which was a costume decorated as a snooker table, complete with cues, balls and pockets.

## LANE, LUPINO – HENRY GEORGE LUPINO

An English comedian and singer, Lupino (1892–1959) was a member of the Lupino family, which was connected with Panto for 200 years.

## LEMON, MARK

As well as a journalist, Mark Lemon was an English writer of some of the most successful Pantos to be presented on the Victorian stage.

## LESLIE, FANNY

Fanny Leslie (1857–1935) was an English actress who was one of the most popular Principal Boys of the late Victorian Panto.

## LITTLE TICH – HARRY RELPH

Standing at just 4ft tall, Little Tich (1867–1928) became one of the great stars of music hall, Burlesque and of course Panto. He included impersonations, eccentric dancing in huge boots and various songs in his act and became a major attraction in the celebrated Drury Lane Pantos of the 1890s.

## LLOYD, MARIE – MATILDA ALICE VICTORIA WOOD

As a singer, Marie Lloyd (1870–1922) has been hailed as one of the greatest of all music hall stars in the 1880s. She subsequently became a popular Panto actress at Drury Lane Theatre and elsewhere. Some though said that her bawdy and somewhat risqué humour was not best suited to Panto.

## LUPINO FAMILY

The Lupino family is a famous English theatrical family which enjoyed an almost uninterrupted association with the world of Panto from its inception through to the twenty-first century. Members of this family claim descent from a line of Italian puppeteers and were first seen on the English stage shortly after the Restoration.

## MELVILLE BROTHERS

Walter (1875–1937) and Frederick Melville (1879–1938) were English theatre managers and authors who wrote and staged numerous successful Pantos at the Lyceum Theatre, which together they managed from 1909 until 1938.

## MORELY, JOHN

John Morely is an English actor and writer of Pantos who as a result was dubbed the 'King of Panto' and each year there are literally hundreds of his Pantos playing throughout the UK.

## PAYNE, W.H.

An English actor famous for his performances in Panto during the mid-Victorian era, Payne (1804–78) made his debut in 1825 and quickly established himself as a fine actor.

## POVEY, ELIZA

Eliza Povey (1804–61) was an English actress who is thought to have been one of the first (if not the *very* first), female performers to take the role of Principal Boy as early as 1819 in the English Panto, a claim that is actually supported by records to that effect.

## RANDALL, HARRY

Harry Randall (1860–1932) was the actor/singer and close friend of Dan Leno who became the successor to Leno when he died, thereafter playing Panto Dame himself at Drury Lane until his own retirement in 1913.

# RICH, JOHN

English actor and theatre manager John Rich (1681–1761) is frequently described as the 'Father of Panto'. Upon his father's death, he and his brother inherited control of the Lincoln's Inn Fields Theatre. Spurred on by the success of Drury Lane Theatre, a 'Panto War' ensued between the management of the two theatres. The first Rich production which was billed as a Panto was *Harlequin Sorcerer* in 1717. It was a huge success and was followed by a continuous flow of successes over the next forty years.

# ROBEY, SIR GEORGE (EDWARD) – GEORGE EDWARD

One of the most popular stars of music hall and Panto, George (1869–1954) was an English comedian and singer and nicknamed the 'Prime Minister of Mirth'. His first appearance in Panto was in 1899 when he played one of the Babes in *Babes in the Wood* and graduated from there to become one of the most successful Dames of his time.

# THOMPSON, LYDIA

Lydia Thmpson (1836–1908) was an English actress who was known for playing the part of Principal Boy in Victorian Pantos.

# TRIPP, JACK

One of the most popular Dames to tread the boards in the post-war era was the nationally celebrated Jack Tripp (1922–2005).

# VESTRIS, MADAME – LUCY ELIZABETH BARTOLOZZI

Madame Vestris (1797–1856) was a theatre manager, actress and singer who was one of the first notable Principal Boys.

So now we know Who's Who, let's find out more about What's What. In this section you may come across some words or terms that perhaps you have heard before but never truly understood, and perhaps some may be completely new to you too. Many of these terms and what they stand for are, of course, now confined to the Panto and theatrical archives – but that doesn't mean that we can, or indeed should, forget them because it is history that creates the present and the present which shapes the future.

# WHAT?

## ABRACADABRA

This is a popular word with all children because it generally means that magic is about to take place.

## AD LIB

This means to make up one's own lines on the spur of the moment. It is a particularly useful skill to have for Panto actors/actresses, due to the unpredictability of Panto – with the encouragement of audience participation, one never knows in what direction the performance will go and so it is left up to the skills of the actor to bring the wandering show back on track.

## AWKWARD SQUAD

The marvellous comedy scene which involves the Dame of the Panto and 'her' hilarious attempts to marshal a group of incompetent volunteers or troops into an efficient fighting force which will eventually march against the enemy; sometimes members of the audience are even drafted into the scene.

## BASHING THE BABY

This is a traditional and knock-about routine that is now considered rather distasteful and non-PC, with the result that it is no longer seen in annual Pantos. It was one of the most well known of Joseph Grimaldi's comedy routines, surviving even Grimaldi himself and was made up of a series of gags during which the clown mistreated a baby by taking the usual feeding and cleaning routines to the extreme; an example would be that the baby was fed with a giant ladle instead of a tiny spoon and washed in boiling water and then dried by being put through a wringer. Public outrage during the late Victorian era brought the routine to an end.

## BRISTLE TRAP

Traps are frequently used in Pantos and a bristle trap is just one in the family of traps. The entrance to a bristle trap is usually concealed by the use of overlapping bristles or foliage through which a performer (character) can make a surprise and unexpected appearance, taking the audience unawares.

## CARPENTER'S SCENE

This is a sparsely set scene that takes place in front of the front cloth, whilst behind the cloth the stage crew are then able to change the scenery on the main stage. Quite often it is during this scene that the audience participation song takes place.

## CATCHPHRASES

Panto has given birth to many catchphrases over the years and some of these are listed below.

| | |
|---|---|
| *'Ain't he like our Fred?'*<br>*'Get your hair cut.'*<br>*'Go and cut yourself a piece of cake.'* | These are three of the popular catchphrases that were called out by the audience in the early part of the twentieth century, not only on the entrance of a particular character but also when they thought the comedy was flagging; very subtle! |
| *'Here we are again.'* | A traditional cry by the clown as he enters. The first to utter these words was Joseph Grimaldi. |
| *'New lamps for old.'* | The cry of Abanazar in the Panto *Aladdin*. |
| *'Oh yes it is –<br>oh no it isn't'* | Another of the more well-known Panto catchphrases which takes the form of banter between one of the characters on the stage and the audience. |
| *'Open Sesame.'* | This particular catchphrase is from the Panto *Aladdin*. |
| *'He's behind you.'* | Probably one of the most well-known of all the Panto catchphrases called out when one of the Goodies fails to see one of the Baddies standing right behind him/them. |

Then there are popular catchphrases that have been carried into Panto on the back of popular performers of the day, some of which are given below.

| | |
|---|---|
| *'Can you hear me, mother?'* | The catchphrase that Sandy Powell famously called out to his audiences. |
| *'Hello playmates!'* | This was Arthur Askey's greeting to his expectant audience. |
| *'I'm free!'* | John Inman took this catchphrase into Panto with him from the hit TV show *Are You Being Served?* in which he was one of the stars. |
| *'Wotcher!'* | Danny La Rue's personal and well-known catchphrase which he used in Pantos across the country. |

## CHASE SCENE

This is the traditional slapstick scene in a Panto in which characters are engaged in riotous pursuit, where everything is spilt, broken or knocked over and where characters collide with both each other and any other object or person in their path. The chase scene is often choreographed in the manner of the silent movies of the early twentieth century and can spill over into the Panto audience too (ironically the films had been influenced by Pantos).

## CORNER TRAP

Stage trap that is positioned downstage right and/or left through which the supernatural Goodies and Baddies can magically appear and disappear.

## CORSICAN TRAP

This is a form of the ghost glide, and the ghost glide is a variety of trap that enables a performer to appear as though he/she is gliding across the stage when in fact they are actually being carried across on a wheeled platform running under the stage.

## DIORAMA

This is an elaborate back-cloth used in mid-nineteenth-century Pantos. It was gradually unfurled across the stage to display an ever changing panoramic view.

## DOWN TRAP

This variety of the trap enabled an actor to appear as though he had just dived through a solid stage floor with the mouth of the trap being hidden by a mat which would spring back into place after the actor had passed through the floor; he would then be caught by a blanket below the stage.

## FALLING FLAP

This is a hinged flap, painted on both sides, which is fitted onto flats on the stage – or other scenic items on the stage for that matter – which when released in any variety of directions can facilitate an almost instantaneous transformation of the setting, thus creating a new scene. They are also used to transform one object into another such as a box into a table, etc.

The current Health and Safety laws in force today prevent many of these traps being used in productions, but it is good to know how, in times gone by, effects were created for the audiences without the sophistication of today's technology.

## FEE-FI-FO-FUM

These are the words called out by the Giant in *Jack and the Beanstalk* whenever he thinks he can detect the presence of Jack. In its entirety the call is:

> *Fee-fi-fo-fum,*
> *I smell the blood of an Englishman;*
> *Be he live or be he dead,*
> *I'll grind his bones to make my bread.*

## FLAG

This was the name given to the board that carried the song sheet for the audience participation sing-a-long. It used to be a signboard used for carrying the words not just of a song but of dialogue too at a time when venues other than the Patent Theatres were prevented from staging spoken drama by the Licensing Act of 1737. It was generally lowered from the flies or even carried on by the performers themselves.

## FOREPIECE (OR CURTAIN RAISER)

This was a piece of entertainment – even a play – presented at the beginning of an evening's entertainment, prior to the Panto. Originally, Panto was only one part of an evening's entertainment, although its popularity grew to such an extent that it eventually became the entire evening's entertainment.

## GHOST SCENE

This is a traditional Panto scene and is used as a comic interlude in which the Dame, for example, is frequently found in a gloomy and haunted room with only ghostly spirits for company.

## HAYMARKET

This is a theatre in London which was once famous for its Pantos which were staged here regularly in the nineteenth century.

## JOEY

Joey is the traditional name given to all clowns in honour of that great clown Joseph Grimaldi and the comic business in a Panto is often referred to as Joey-Joey in his memory.

## LAUNDRY SCENE

This very popular and traditional chase scene can be found in the Panto *Aladdin*, where Aladdin is pursued through his mother's laundry by the two Chinese Policemen, and sometimes even Aladdin's mother herself. When permitted, the use of traps frequently heightens the excitement for the children in the audience as the characters appear, disappear and are propelled hither and thither as Aladdin attempts to escape.

## LINCOLN'S INN FIELDS THEATRE

This is a former theatre that was situated in Portugal Street, London and was the birthplace of Panto. It was where, in the early eighteenth century, John Rich staged the first Panto.

## LONDON PALLADIUM

This famous theatrical landmark stands in Argyll Street, London and became famous for its annual Panto after the Second World War. It was at this theatre that Dame Anna Neagle made her last Panto appearance. To this day, an appearance at the London Palladium is still considered to be the pinnacle of a performer's career.

## MAGIC BEANS

These are the beans that Idle Jack is given in exchange for his mother's cow and which subsequently sprout into a giant beanstalk. It is this beanstalk that Jack climbs to reach the Giant's castle above the clouds.

## OLIO

This is a selection of miscellaneous scenes from several different productions which are, for want of another word, 'cobbled' together to make an evening's entertainment. Panto Olios were regularly presented on tour in the Provinces in the early nineteenth century.

## PEPPER'S GHOST

This technique is an arrangement of mirrors to create the illusion of a ghost walking on the stage amongst real characters. The illusion was actually a reflection of an actor walking in the pit. The great Joseph Grimaldi was known for his performances in just such a scene.

## RISE-AND-SINK

Way back in the nineteenth century this was the means by which Panto sets were transformed almost instantaneously. The effect worked when the upper half of a set of flats – or other scenic item – was quickly drawn up into the flies, whilst the lower half was carried down by a slot into the cellar, thus revealing new scenery standing immediately behind.

## ROLL-OUT

This is a concealed opening in a flat through which a performer can make a sudden surprise entrance.

## SCHOOLROOM SCENE

This is a scene that has its history in the *commedia dell'arte*, involving the comedy characters together with a chorus of rowdy children in a battle with a teacher, who is usually the Dame. Generally, the scene involves a blackboard, lots of complicated sums, schoolboy howlers and slapstick routines.

## SKIN PARTS

This is a term used to describe the role of an animal played on stage, where the actors/actresses must dress in skins to play the part. Such roles/animals in Panto include:

• Camel in *Aladdin*
• Cat in *Dick Whittington*
• Cat in *Puss in Boots*
• Goose in *Mother Goose*
• Cow in *Jack and the Beanstalk*
• Mice in *Cinderella*

## SLAPSTICK

The traditional, noisy and physical comedy scene which has become synonymous with the word Panto itself, and which appears at least once in all good Pantos; there is really little difference between this and a slosh scene, both being just an excuse for as much fun, noise and mess as possible.

## SLOSH SCENE

A traditionally very messy scene where such things as wallpaper and wallpaper paste, pies made of shaving foam pastry, collapsing tables, buckets of water, ladders with ill-fitting rungs, even exploding gas cookers abound to heighten the fun. The children in the audience love it, whilst the adults just pray that they don't try to re-enact it when they get home!

## SLOTE (OR SLOAT)

Developed in the Victorian theatre from earlier versions, this is a stage mechanism which – using an arrangement of counter-weights and rails, allows scenery to rise onto the stage through slots (also called slotes) cut in the stage floor. Aren't we lucky today with all our advanced technology?

## SLOW TRAP

This is a powered trap used to raise and lower performers/scenery up onto or off the stage.

## TRANSFORMATION SCENE OR GRAND TRANSFORMATION

This is traditionally the scene in a Panto in which a spectacular transformation of scene and or characters takes place.

## TREE OF TRUTH

This refers to the magical tree in one of the most famous and traditional comic scenes in Panto. Although not seen as often in the modern Panto as it was in the early part of the twentieth century, occasionally it still does thankfully appear now and again to the delight of the excited children in the audience. It works like this. The Tree of Truth is usually heavy with a good crop of fruit which right on cue falls onto the head of anyone who sits under the tree and tells a lie – a sort of lie detector I suppose!

## VAMP TRAP

Formally called a vampire trap, this is a hinged trap that gives performers the ability to look as though they are able to appear or disappear through a solid stage floor.

Okay, so now you know Who's Who and What's What, we can move onto where things are or came from, because let's face it something you cannot find or locate is of very little use to you, is it now!

# WHERE?

## BOWERY THEATRE

We British like to think that Panto is all ours, and it is to some extent! However, there once existed a theatre in New York which was renowned for staging Pantos and that is – was – the Bowery Theatre. It was famous for something else too, and that is fire! This ill-fated theatre actually burned down in 1828, 1836 and 1845. It was renamed the Old Bowery Theatre in 1858; maybe someone thought a change of name would secure a change of luck? Still intact, it then closed in 1878 and then reopened as the Thalia Theatre, finally closing permanently in 1929 after – guess what? – two more fires! Maybe America was just not meant to have Pantos. It would certainly have made me think twice, I can tell you, before buying a ticket for a Panto – at least at this particular theatre.

## ENTRANCES

It is traditional in Panto Land that good characters, such as the Fairy Godmother, make their entrance from the right and usually in a white or pink lighting state, whilst the evil characters, such as the Demon King, make their entrances from the left and usually in a green lighting state.

## FLIES

This is the name given to the area above the stage from which the flymen can fly the lighting equipment and scenery. The area is fitted out with catwalks and bars for ease of movement.

## FRONT OF HOUSE

The Front of House can be found exactly where the name suggests at the front of the house, (theatre), and includes areas such as the foyer and the bars. In charge, again as one would expect, is the Front of House Manager.

Now the location section is duly over we can conclude with when things actually happened in this magical world they call Panto Land.

# WHEN?

Things just don't happen, they evolve and grow. Here you will find a list of some of the signposts and high points in the development and growth of Panto, with the accent on the word some.

| Time | Event |
|------|-------|
| First century | The word Panto is used for the first time, although it had little to do with today's Panto for it referred to performers of bawdy entertainment in the Roman Empire. |
| Fourteenth century | It was thought unladylike for women to appear on the stage and so men dressed as women for the female parts – perhaps this was the beginning of the Panto Dame! Acceptance of female actresses was actually a very slow progression and even when it was accepted that a woman may indeed be permitted to tread the boards, it was not until well into the twentieth century that it became a respectable profession for the female sex. |
| 1717 | *The Loves of Mars and Venus*, a Ballet-Panto, is staged by John Weaver and is the first production to be actually billed as a Panto. |
| 1717 | John Rich stages a series of new-style productions – Pantos. |
| 1773 | In this year the first performance of *Jack the Giant Killer* was staged as a Christmas play at Drury Lane. (This was the forerunner of the Panto *Jack and the Beanstalk*.) |
| 1788 | The very first production of the Panto *Aladdin*. |
| 1800 | This is the year in which Joseph Grimaldi made his first appearance as Clown. |
| 1804 | The first performance of *Cinderella*. |
| 1814 | *Dick Whittington* makes a debut performance. |
| 1818 | First performance of *Puss in Boots*. |
| 1819 | The year of the first performance of *Jack and the Beanstalk*. |
| 1823 | The theatrical world says goodbye to the great Joseph Grimaldi who is forced to retire from his regular appearances through ill health. |
| 1828 | It is in this year that Grimaldi makes two farewell performances. |

| | |
|---|---|
| 1830 | Great changes are afoot when Madame Vestris becomes the first woman to manage a London Theatre – the Olympic Theatre. |
| 1831 | A production of *Mother Goose* crosses the pond to New York but the American audiences 'don't get it' and so the production fails. |
| 1837 | Joseph Grimaldi dies. |
| 1843 | The Theatre Regulation Act. |
| 1844 | The first performance of a Panto by E.L. Blanchard, who later became known as the 'Prince of Openings'. |
| 1850s | It was not until the mid-nineteenth century that Pantos became known as a form of Christmas entertainments. |
| 1861 | The first performance of *Aladdin*. |
| 1869 | Enter the Vokes family who were all set to rule over the Panto scene for ten years at Drury Lane. |
| 1870s | Pantos grow in popularity, as does the running time which can be as much as 3 hours – imagine a twenty-first-century child content to leave their computerised games for that length of time to sit and watch live theatre! Panto itself was becoming ever more of an extravaganza, which annoyed many. |
| 1886 | Saw the first appearance of the celebrated Dan Leno (who it is considered created the modern day Panto Dame) when he played the Dame in *Jack and the Beanstalk*. |
| 1900s | During the first half of the twentieth century the true tradition of Panto as we know it today was growing and evolving through the courage of various producers who were willing to experiment with the different forms. |
| 1948 | After the war years the London Palladium surfaced as the leading home of the modern Panto. |
| 1950s | The next decade saw the rise of the male celebrity cast in the role of the Dame. |
| 1960s | By this time most homes in the UK had a television set and so it made financial sense to bring the stars of the small screen to the stage, whilst at the same time enticing the curious non theatre-goer into the theatre, if only on an annual basis. |

| | |
|---|---|
| 1970s | Females playing the Principal Boy in Panto had been in decline since the rise and popularity of males playing the Dame, but in the 1970s it became apparent that there was a place for two cross-dressing acts in one show and so the popularity of the female Principal Boy increased once more. |
| 1980s | The decline of the big spectacular Pantos but the growth of the Provincial Pantos. |
| 1990s | Panto continues to flourish without major changes. London, though, is no longer the home of this form of theatre with generally only one or very few productions each year. But provincial theatres nationwide are beginning to take over and can be relied upon to stage their annual Panto, often starring at least one major celebrity. Then, the amateur companies regularly also stage their own Panto with some companies in existence solely for this purpose – and so in true theatrical |

The young 'Babes' pose with the professionals, perhaps hoping that one day they too will be professional performers having served their apprenticeship in this unique and special way.

|  | tradition resting for the remainder of the year! Panto, though, still hasn't conquered America, but there's time … Oh yes there is! |
|---|---|
| 2000s | We have reached the new Millennium where bigger and better TVs dominate most living rooms. For this reason, the success of a Panto has come to rely very much upon the importance and popularity of the soap stars the producers contract to appear in their productions. |

## DANCE – WHY IS DANCE INCLUDED IN A PANTO?

Dance is one of those art forms that many of us look upon in awe; I mean just how does one individual manage to get his/her leg in some of the most seemingly inaccessible of places? Well, inaccessible to legs anyway! And what's more with such grace too. Dance is just so beautiful to watch; it is artistic, it is graceful and, when performed as an integral part of theatre, it even tells a story too.

Dance is an immensely important part of Panto. Why? Well, quite simply because it is one of the elements that pulls in the children, both as performers and as audience members. Most little girls go to dance classes at some point in their lives and it is from the local dance schools that both the professional and amateur Panto production companies recruit their child dancers – traditionally called Panto Babes – to take a part in their productions. It is oh so exciting for the children who are chosen to be a Babe, and exciting for their families, and for the other children in the dance school who this year were not lucky enough to be chosen, but whose 'luck' just might change next year. This all equates to promoting arts education for the very young, for children on the stage and in the audience are, after all, tomorrow's dedicated theatre-goers.

Another contribution Panto dancers, and indeed Panto itself, makes to the arts is by the very fact that the 'older' dancers are generally recruited from the larger and nationally renowned professional, performing arts schools, such as Arts Educational in London and PPA in Guildford, as indeed are many of the minor or supporting roles too such as, Peter Pan in *Peter Pan* or Princess Jasmine in *Aladdin*. In other words, the professional world of Panto provides the theatre-goer with high-class entertainment, usually featuring current soap stars, and introduces them to the stars of tomorrow, who can often be found playing the minor roles, as well as enticing in the younger children, both on and off the stage, through the roles of the dancing Babes and the exciting audience participation. Yes, Panto is both an entertainer and an educator.

## WHO CREATES DANCE FOR PANTO?

The answer to that question is, of course, quite simple and straightforward. I have always had enormous respect for those who choreograph Pantos, and for very good reasons too, for these are experienced and talented artistes in their own right, as one will see below. They are the ones who are known for their innovative and exciting choreography in the world of musical theatre and/or commercial theatre. And, so it is that each year top-class producers bring in and book top-class choreographers to choreograph their Pantos, knowing that if they book the best, then they will get the best – and they do. They get the best because these talented individuals devise and create choreography to suit the cast of the show and not to show off their own enormous talents. They may be asked to work with the most well-known and talented of actors/actresses but often these actors/actresses have never danced a step in their lives and yet the choreographers somehow manage to make them look like the next Darcey Bussell – well, okay then, perhaps 'almost' like the next Darcey Bussell! And then when they have finished climbing that particular artistic mountain, they prepare for their ascent of the next, and that is the one of teaching the Babes, who are often more concerned with the nearest toilet or the nearest vending machine than with the next step in a routine! But in the end who doesn't think that Panto Babes are the cutest ever? And as one who has seen some troupes of Babes where each seems to be a left-footed centipede, then let me assure you that this is quite often thanks to the choreographer who creates the perfect routine for their dance teachers to instil into them, so that they eventually evolve into a troupe of dancing angels. You know, all artists like to stretch themselves artistically and to show off their most creative and best work, but a Panto choreographer cannot do that for they must create work that will show off others and for that I take my hat off to them! Now, let me introduce you to two of the UK's leading and most respected Panto choreographers – Barbara (Babs) Evans and Gerry Zuccarello.

## BARBARA (BABS) EVANS, DIRECTOR/CHOREOGRAPHER

- Barbara Evans was born in Leigh Lancashire, the daughter of Teresa and John Evans
- She has an older brother, David who, as a die-hard Manchester United fan, was to prove very useful to Barbara later in her professional life
- As a child and teenager, Barbara danced in the local amateur Pantos with the St Joseph's Players, the oldest amateur dramatic group in the country
- After leaving grammar school she attended Elliott-Clarke's College in Liverpool before going on to London College of Dance and Drama
- Barbara's first professional performance was in *Joseph and his Technicolor Dreamcoat* at the Liverpool Playhouse, whilst she was still at college
- After taking her final teaching exams she became an examiner for the ISTD which lead to overseas lectures and tours
- Working with a team from Finland, she choreographed the winning entry for the World Show Dance Championships in 1993
- It was in 1994 that she started choreographing professionally, though really her first ever piece was *Sleeping Beauty* at the age of 7!
- It was also in 1994 that Barbara choreographed her first professional Panto, *Aladdin*, at the Hexagon Theatre in Reading, for Nick Thomas, who was later to become head of Qdos
- She later entered the artistic world of circus performance when she started creating unique performance spectaculars for Chessington World of Adventures in Surrey. Here she combined high-level artistes within a themed format (similar to Cirque du Soleil)
- In 2000 Barbara started her directing career with *Peter Pan*, a show she has recreated every year since for Qdos Entertainment, working alongside David Essex and Paul Nicholas
- In addition, she has also choreographed several musicals, including *Grease* and *Little Shop of Horrors*

- In 2002 she was booked by Paul Elliot to choreograph her most successful musical to date, *I Keano*, at the Olympia Theatre in Dublin as well as for other venues throughout Southern Ireland; *I Keano* is a musical comedy about the fateful Football World Cup in which Roy Keane had an enormous row with the manager, Mick McCarthy. It was here that her brother David's obsession with Manchester United was to come in very useful as he gave her insight into the event!
- Despite her success, she continues to choreograph Pantos each year – for it seems that once this bug has bitten it is hard to shake off
- Barbara Evans is now a nationally renowned choreographer and director who, since those early childhood days of dancing in Pantos herself, has gone on to choreograph nineteen professional Pantos and direct a further twelve; all this in addition to her innumerate and extensive choreographic and directing commitments, which continue to grow each year

## AND FINALLY

- Barbara Evans' work has evolved to cover a wide spectrum from bespoke circus shows to musicals as well as commercial pop/rock tours
- After attending the Stageone Producer's Workshop and the Central School of Acting Business Bootcamp, Barbara took the decision to concentrate on show development and as a consequence began working on production development with various European companies, so beginning a new chapter in her already highly successful career

## GERRY ZUCCARELLO, DANCER, CHOREOGRAPHER AND DIRECTOR

- Gerry was born in Dorking Surrey on 24 February 1963, the first son of Angela and Fedele Zucarrello. Gerry has a younger brother, Mario
- As his name suggests, he is of Italian decent and as a result is bilingual
- The Zuccarello family now live in Reigate, Surrey
- Gerry was educated at St Joseph's Primary School and later at St Bede's

Secondary School in Redhill where he excelled at all things practical. Together with his brother, Mario, as a child Gerry had a passion for taking apart anything and everything, just to see how it worked, only to put it back together again; this is a passion that he retains to this day

- In 1971, at the age of 8 years old, he started dancing classes at Laine Theatre Arts in Surrey, where he discovered he had a natural talent for dance, and so this, it turned out, was a decision that was to shape his life for ever
- After leaving full-time education in 1979, Gerry was offered, and accepted, a place on the full-time dancers' course at Laine Theatre Arts in Surrey from, where he graduated three years later
- His first professional job was as a dancer on the Lena Zavaroni Show in 1982
- In 1989 he met his future wife, Carol, who was also a dancer
- In September 1990, after a highly successful career as a professional dancer, Gerry Zuccarello returned to his roots when he became a dance teacher at Laine Theatre Arts, where it all began
- In 1992 Gerry and Carol married and went on to have two daughters, Chiara and Gavina
- It was in 1995 that Gerry entered the world of Panto when he choreographed his first pantomime, *Robinson Crusoe*, at the Theatre Royal, Newcastle. Since that date he has gone on to choreograph more than thirty-seven pantomimes and is still counting!
- In 1997 Gerry won the Carl-Alan Teachers Award for Stage, Ballet, Tap and Modern
- Alongside his teaching career, where he takes delight in nurturing a new generation of talent, Gerry Zuccarello has also managed to continue his professional work
- In 2004 Gerry choreograph *The Royal Gala Show* for the New Welsh Millennium Centre in Cardiff, which was televised by BBC Wales
- In 1998 he was choreographer on *The Last Salute*, a comedy series for the BBC
- In 1998 he staged *Bouncers* at the Mercury Theatre, Colchester
- In the period 1997–9 he was appointed choreographer for Carl Davies and the Royal Philharmonic and Liverpool Philharmonic Orchestras for their summer concerts and for a charity gala show at the Birmingham Symphony Hall

- Between 2003 and 2005 he was choreographer on the TV specials *Greasemania*, *Abbamania 2*, *Madonna-mania*, *Elvismania* and *Discomania 2* for LWT/Granada TV
- Between 2007 and 2009 he choreographed the Entertainment Artistes' Benevolent Fund annual gala at the London Palladium
- In 2010 Gerry was appointed Artistic Director and Choreographer for Voyage of Discovery Cruise Line
- Christmas 2013/14 saw Gerry at the Theatre Royal, Nottingham for the second year in succession, this time as choreographer for the Pantomime *Peter Pan*
- Along with several star names, he is currently involved in the planning of a large charity concert for Cancer Research; the event is scheduled to take place in the spring of 2014

## AND FINALLY

- Gerry has over 1,000 TV credits to his name, including six Royal Command performances
- He has worked for a variety of TV companies, both here and overseas, including BBC, LWT, Sky TV, TV Asia, Italian, German, Belgian and Dutch TV
- He has also staged numerous plays, choreographed three musicals and seven pop videos
- Gerry Zuccarello has had a full, exciting and non-stop career as a dancer and choreographer, and yet insists that his greatest achievements are his two delightful daughters, who themselves are world-class Irish Dancers, having qualified for the world championships several years in succession

## WELL, I NEVER KNEW THAT!

No matter how much you thought you knew, there's always something else – something you didn't know, you didn't know

- Douglas Byng's stage career spanned an amazing seven decades
- There is money in stupidity after all as was proved in the 2007 Panto production of *Aladdin* at the Birmingham Hippodrome. This Panto apparently grossed in excess of £1,750,000

- In Skegness one teenage schoolgirl laughed so hard at the foolish antics of Norman Wisdom in Panto that she dislocated her jaw
- It was, in part, thanks to Rex Harrison that Norman Wisdom pursued a career in the entertainment industry for after Harrison saw Wisdom perform in a charity show, he suggested that he take up the profession as a career, and thank goodness he did too. Without Norman Wisdom not only would the entertainment industry be a poorer place, but Panto itself would never have been the same without the unique contribution of this slapstick, comedic genius
- The name Buttons – as the character in the Panto *Cinderella* – originated from page boys who were nicknamed Buttons because their uniforms had rows of buttons sewn onto them. And if you think about it Buttons' costume is that of a page boy with rows of buttons sewn onto it
- The Principal Boy in a Panto is traditionally played by a girl and is known in Panto Land as 'the breeches part'
- *Mother Goose* is sometimes called the 'Grand-Daddy' of Pantos in that it is probably one of the oldest tales to be adapted into a Panto, for it dates back to an Ancient Greek legend about a goose that laid golden eggs
- 'Here we are again' is the traditional cry of a clown on making his entrance
- Each year on the first Sunday in February, clowns from all over the UK gather together in Dalston (East London) in order to attend a church service which is held in memory of the clown Joseph Grimaldi. This annual tradition has been going on since 1946. In 1959 the annual memorial service moved to Holy Trinity Church and it was in 1967 that permission was given for the clowns attending, to do so in full clown regalia
- It is said that the Ghost of Dan Leno, one of the original great Panto Dames, still puts in an appearance at Drury Lane. Not sure about that being a laughing matter, though
- Tchaikovsky wrote the ballet *Sleeping Beauty* in 1890, whilst Walt Disney made the cartoon version in 1958
- As many as 3,000 people would see each Panto performance of the great Joseph Grimaldi, meaning that approximately one-eighth of the population of London at that time witnessed each of his stage roles
- A new record was created in 1806 when Thomas Dibdin's *Mother Goose* ran for 111 nights at Covent Garden

- The page-boy character of Buttons in the Panto *Cinderella* was originally created by the Panto writer H.J. Byron
- It is an unwritten rule that a clown never copies the make-up of another clown, thus making each clown unique.
- Apply the numbers game to Danny La Rue and you will find that: he was in show business for over sixty years, and in over fifty of those years he appeared in over forty-five Pantos. He also starred in one of the longest running Pantos ever known at the Old Saville Theatre, called *Queen Passionella and the Sleeping Beauty*
- In 1856 the role of Lady Badroubaldour, the Emperor of China's daughter in the Panto *Aladdin*, was once played by a man on stilts in a version that opened at the Royal Princess's Theatre
- One of the most celebrated Panto Dames in recent years is the great classical actor Sir Ian McKellen, who played Widow Twankey in the London Old Vic's version of *Aladdin*
- Pantomime at the start of the current decade was accounting for approximately 20 per cent of all live performances, and approximately the same percentage of work for actors in live entertainments occurring between the months of December and March

## SO, WHERE DOES IT ALL BEGIN?

*At the beginning, of course, with pantomime roadshows.*

So, we have seen the best of Panto and those who inhabit the land of talking animals and mystery. We have established that Panto's important role in theatre is not only to amuse and entertain, but to open the door of the bigger theatrical experience, as it does oh so well and successfully, year after year. That's good, but have you given any thought to who entices our younger ones to the Panto in the first instance? Well, that would be the parents and families of our little ones, of course; and that is wonderful and how it should be. But there is in fact more, something bigger, brighter and hugely exciting; something and someone from the actual Land itself, and that is the unique *Pantomime Roadshow*, a roadshow run by a Panto Dame and which actually goes out to the children and allows them to enjoy a hands-on experience of this special art form themselves; lets them have such a wonderful time that they cannot wait to get to that theatre and see the real thing for themselves. And it's all there for them in Nigel Ellacott's *Pantomime Roadshow* which he takes to them in the safe and supportive environment of their very own primary school.

This unique and very special *Pantomime Roadshow* tours schools throughout the UK, the intention being to introduce children to the magic of live theatre, and especially to Panto. Nigel has devised an interactive programme aimed at Key Stage Two primary school children which will both entertain and educate them. The children learn all about the history of Pantomime as well as about the intriguing traditions surrounding it too. They have the fun of watching the show before being an part of it when they are not only shown the costumes but when some are actually allowed to dress up in them too; they handle the props and see the scenery close up as they become totally involved in the experience. This is theatre at its very best and Nigel Ellacott and his Roadshow team play to ten schools a week, which can mean as many as 3,000 children a week – or more!

This exciting presentation concludes with a question and answer session and who better to answer questions than an expert on the art of Pantomime – Nigel Ellacott himself. I do believe that not only does Panto owe a great debt to him, but so too does the entire world of theatre, for he is opening the door to the greater theatrical experience that so many of us have spent a lifetime enjoying …because panto is where theatre begins.

## THE END

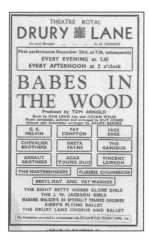

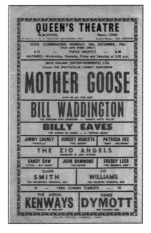

# BIBLIOGRAPHY

Cookman, L., *How to Write a Pantomime*, Accent Press Ltd, 2007

Hudd, R., *A Fart in a Colander*, Michael O'Mara Books Ltd, 2009

Kennedy, D. (ed.), *Oxford Companion to Theatre and Performance*, Oxford University, 2011

Mellor, G.J., *They Made Us Laugh*, George Kelsall, 2009

Crystal, David (ed.), *Penguin Concise Encyclopaedia*, 3rd edn, Penguin Reference Library, 2007

Pickering, D., *Encyclopaedia of Pantomime*, Gale Research International Ltd, 1993

## NEWSPAPERS AND PERIODICALS

*Guardian*
*Daily Mail*
*Stage*

## WEBSITES

Melvyn Hayes' official website
www.its-behind-you.com

## OTHER SOURCES

BBC News Channel

# INDEX

# Discover Your History

## Ancestors • Heritage • Memories

Each issue of *Discover Your History* presents special features and regular articles on a huge variety of topics about our social history and heritage – such as our ancestors, childhood memories, military history, British culinary traditions, transport history, our rural and industrial past, health, houses, fashions, pastimes and leisure ... and much more.

Historic pictures show how we and our ancestors have lived and the changing shape of our towns, villages and landscape in Britain and beyond.

Special tips and links help you discover more about researching family and local history. Spotlights on fascinating museums, history blogs and history societies also offer plenty of scope to become more involved.

Keep up to date with news and events that celebrate our history, and reviews of the latest books and media releases.

*Discover Your History* presents aspects of the past partly through the eyes and voices of those who were there.

*Discover Your History* is in all good newsagents and also available on subscription for six or twelve issues. For more details on how to take out a subscription and how to choose your free book, call 01778 392013 or visit **www.discoveryourhistory.net**

**FREE BOOK**
WHEN YOU SUBSCRIBE TO
*Discover Your History*

UK only

## OTHER BOOKS BY
## MAUREEN HUGHES

*The Pocket Guide to Musicals*
ISBN: 978 1 84468 039 9
£9.99

*The Pocket Guide to Plays and Playwrights*
ISBN: 978 1 84468 043 6
£12.99

*The Pocket Guide to Classic Books*
ISBN: 978 1 84468 061 0
£14.99

*The Pocket Guide to Ballroom Dancing*
ISBN: 978 1 84468 082 5
£9.99